BARK

Cédric Pollet

BARK

An Intimate Look at the World's Trees

F

FRANCES LINCOLN LIMITED

PUBLISHERS

The origins of a love affair

I was born in Nice, a region of France that abounds with a lush natural beauty, made even more alluring by that subtle quality of light that artists love so much. My family's roots are in two different regions of France – the Mediterranean on my mother's side and the Savoy on my father's. This particular combination gave me, from the very earliest age, the chance to get to know the world of trees: the olive trees, umbrella pines, eucalyptus and other exotics of my mother's part of the world and the larches, spruces, beech trees and silver birches of my father's. My deep-seated passion for plants found its first actual expression while I was studying for my degree in agricultural engineering at Lyon. In 1999, I had the opportunity to study in the Landscape Design Department at Reading University. It was during that time that, full of enthusiasm for English gardens, I first taught myself to take pictures using the classic silver-process photography technique. After spending a lot of time visiting gardens in search of what I hoped would be my ideal subject, I realised one day that flowers didn't really do much for me. But I couldn't leave without some kind of souvenir. On my way out of that garden, the gnarled trunk of a centuries-old oak tree caught my attention and literally opened my eyes to a hitherto unknown domain: the world of bark. It turned out to be a revelation that changed the course of my life. Several months later, returning to my native Cote d'Azur, I began to take notice of the trees in its avenues, parks and public gardens; it felt as if I were visiting my home town for the first time. Before then I had been blinded by the brilliantly exuberant displays of bougainvillea, lagerstroemias and oleanders; after that visit, my ideas underwent a radical change of direction. The ubiquitous plane trees, relegated in so many towns to the role of background street furniture, turned into a source of never-ending inspiration for me; my new-found love for its bark encouraged me to travel far afield – to the terraces of paddy fields and the high mountain lakes – in my efforts to capture images of it. From that moment on, I felt that native trees, be they planes, strawberry trees, white poplars or pines, were just as interesting as their rivals from foreign lands – eucalyptus, monkey puzzle trees, the cajeput, banana trees, palms and so on. In fact, the idea of seeing trees in their native habitat began to interest me more and more. Still, it would have been hard to imagine then that my sudden and inexplicable attraction to bark would become, just a few years later, my future career. I put together a photographic exhibition for my father's birthday, consisting solely of assembled photographs I had taken of bark. This exhibition caught the eye of an art expert who urged me to continue down this path. I finished my last year in the Landscape Department of the National Institute of Horticulture in Angers and on the very day after I had my viva voce for my dissertation, I flew off, camera in hand, for the lands of the dragon and the rising sun. On my return from Asia, I felt inspired to create a dozen new compositions.

Preceding page:
Trunk, *Eucalyptus deglupta*
FAIRCHILD TROPICAL BOTANIC
GARDEN, CORAL
GABLES, FLORIDA (USA)

↖ First eucalyptus
photographed in 1999.
NICE (FRANCE)

↖ *Adenium socotranum*, a giant with an orange trunk.
SOCOTRA (YEMEN)

A few months later, in January 2001, the students' representative body in Nice offered me the chance to exhibit my photographic work. From then on, motivated by the growing enthusiasm the public demonstrated for my bark photographs, more than 50 exhibitions followed not only in France (in Nice, Lyon, Paris and elsewhere), but also in Australia, the United States and in Germany. Supported by awards from the two specialist youth foundations, I got the chance to spend six months discovering the sacred trees of the Maoris, the magical monkey puzzles of New Caledonia, the majestic eucalyptus trees of Australia and the legendary baobab trees of South Africa. These are the trees, and the hundreds more like them, that I have chosen to concentrate on in this book, so that you can share the same intense feelings I experienced when I first saw them.

the Book

This work is first and foremost a homage to the tree. One part of me longs to try to challenge a received idea that has always struck me as questionable: the superiority of the animal world over the world of vegetation. Animals are reactive, and live in the present. Vegetation is pretty much passive, but evolves at its own rhythm, and a much slower one, that of the seasons. Families generally find it more appealing to take their children to the zoo than to a botanic garden to look at trees. At certain special times of the year, however, leaves take on wonderful autumn colours, or flowers put on a spectacular display in the garden or fruits delight our taste buds, and in these short spaces of time, vegetation grabs our attention. So where does bark come into all this? It is pretty much neglected because at first sight it holds little interest for us. You can count books about bark on the fingers of one hand. It is, in fact, present in many forms in our daily lives (cinnamon, cork, rubber, incense, medicines, chewing gums, fibres, pigments and so on), but this only serves to make it seem ordinary. To my mind, it was essential to try to redress this imbalance by helping readers avoid this trap and discover instead a fascinating and unexpected world.

To whet people's enthusiasm, I thought it was important to find ways to surprise and move them, by treating bark in a completely new way, at once aesthetic and playful. The aesthetic potential of bark has no limits and it would be an impossible task to create a definitive book on the subject. For a start, bark is a complex structure that evolves constantly over time. Its inner part is made up of living cells that form the conducting vessels for the sap that travels down from the leaves to all the organs of the tree. The outer layer, made up of dead cells, forms a protective barrier against the onslaught of the outside world. The word bark, as it is

↗ The ageing of the bark of *Araucaria auracaria* over several decades. ʀᴏʏᴀʟ ʙᴏᴛᴀɴɪᴄᴀʟ ɢᴀʀᴅᴇɴs ᴋᴇᴡ, ʀɪᴄʜᴍᴏɴᴅ (ᴜᴋ)

used in this book, covers the outer layer of trees but also that of giant perennials (including palms, bamboos and ferns) whose structure is nevertheless different.

Depending on the species, the bark can stay fixed to the trunk throughout the whole life of the plant or, as it submits to the various forces created by the growth of the tree, it can fold, crack and craze as we see in these photographs of the monkey puzzle tree (*Araucaria araucana*), taken at different stages. Others have a tendency to peel annually in patches, strips and layers in a random and irregular fashion. These are the most interesting ones but also the most difficult to capture. To do this you have to observe dozens of trees of the same species, in different aspects and at different ages, in order to find the most photogenic specimen. The 'snakebark' maple, for example, reveals bark that is much more graphic at the beginning of its growth, compared to the zelkova which does not develop its distinguishing marks until it is an adult tree. So it is important to follow the evolution of the trunk regularly and closely to determine which period of peeling produces the most unexpected colours and changes. From which it follows that it was difficult to take the necessary pictures! The splendid *Arbutus* x *thuretiana* in the garden of the Villa Thuret in Cap d'Antibes illustrates this point perfectly. At the beginning of summer, over the course of a few weeks, the fine, soft bark of this unique shrub goes from orange-red to apple green, then turns rapidly yellow before taking on salmon pink tints.

The photographs of bark printed in this book represent details of trunks largely visible to the naked eye (actual size: minimum of 9cm x 13cm), which is within the grasp of all of us, and they have not been the subject of any kind of colour manipulation. Choosing the 81 tree portraits was extremely difficult. There are about 100,000 different species of tree on our planet. My ten years spent trying to find the most beautiful trees in forests, parks, botanic gardens throughout the world allowed me to amass more than 15,000 images covering around 450 species of plant with remarkable bark. The choice was ultimately made entirely on the grounds of aesthetics (the most graphic, those with the greatest purity of line or the greatest diversity of colour). After that came the criteria of originality, curiosity, rarity, inaccessibility, or usefulness to man. It was also important to show (through the ten montages in this book) the incredible richness of bark in one botanic genus or in one family, my

↖ Following the development of the trunk of *Arubutus* x *thuretiana* over a year.
JARDIN BOTANIQUE DE LA VILLA THURET, INRA ANTIBES (FRANCE)

↗ An experimental plantation of eucalyptus in the Massif de l'Esterel. (FRANCE)

favourites being the eucalyptus and the pines. Although it is not exhaustive, this book offers a great diversity of textures and an exquisite range of natural colours, as good as any rainbow. In total, there are more than 400 photos in this book covering nearly 220 species of tree, classified geographically by continent. This classification has the logic of following where the trees originate from rather than the places where they may be thought to be growing. All the Latin names, in particular the botanic families, have been updated. So don't be surprised to see the maples classified in the *Sapindaceae* family or the baobab or cork in the *Malvaceae*. The text accompanying each image is not intended to be a purely botanical description, since the bark, which is so characteristic, combined with the accompanying photo of the tree, is adequate in most cases to identify the genus or the species. It is primarily light-hearted, with a mixture of anecdotes and ethnic or botanical information that is accessible to everyone.

Besides wanting to share the particular emotions that trees induce in me, the main objective of a book such as this is to make the wider public more aware of the surprising but fragile diversity in the environment we live in. Creating a sense of wonder is, to my mind, the most powerful argument and offers a first step towards gaining respect for such a world. The photographs will seduce, I hope, both art lovers and those who are passionate about nature. The former will concentrate on the purely artistic aspect. The latter will find some useful aids to the identification of some species or, at least, a better understanding of them. With a bit of curiosity and imagination, you can take an unforgettable journey into the intimate world of trees. So open your eyes and take the time to look: the trees will be happy to unveil their secrets to you.

The book is arranged as an imaginary voyage around the world, leaving from Europe and then visiting, one after another, all the continents in which the trees in this book originate.

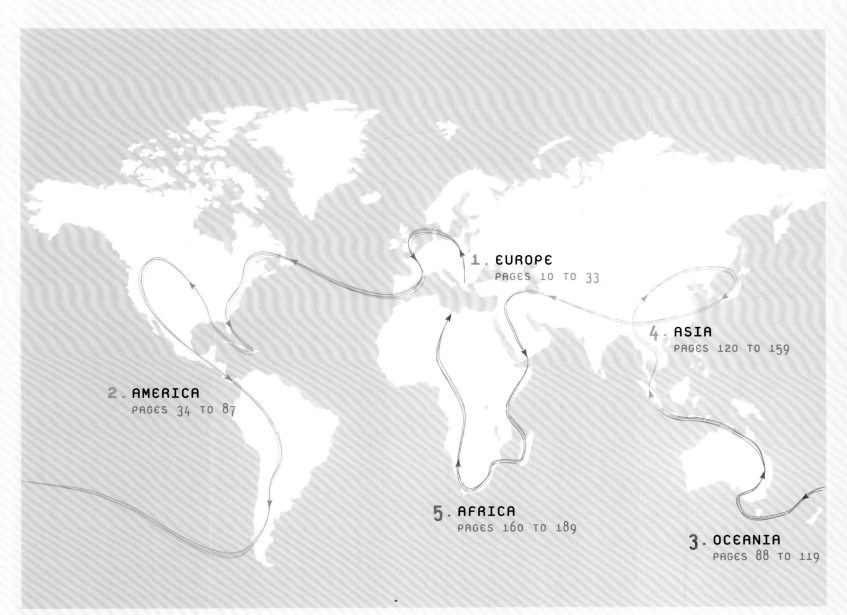

Platanus x hispanica, a remarkable plane tree in a private garden in Lamanon, France.
BOUCHES-DU-RHÔNE
(FRANCE)

SILVER BIRCH

Betula pendula

The silver birch is a pioneering species that has conquered a vast territory, including a good part of Europe, Asia Minor and the western part of Siberia. It is easy to recognize thanks to its thick papery bark, which is ridged and peeling at the base of adult tree trunks. It gets its English name from the silvery colour of its bark and the Latin name *pendula* from its drooping branches. The silver birch is highly prized in Nordic folklore, thanks to its many uses: for writing (paper made from the bark), for shelter (roofing materials), for lighting (torches), for clothing (shoes, belts, perfume) and even for food in times of famine. The wood, which burns well, is highly regarded by both potters and bakers. The sap, harvested in spring and known as 'birch water' is thought to cure rheumatism, urinary infections and skin conditions.

←
→ *Betula pendula*
ROYAL BOTANICAL GARDENS KEW, RICHMOND (UK)

LONDON PLANE

Platanus x *hispanica*

The history of the plane tree dates from the 17th century, the period of the great plant hunting expeditions. Recent genetic research has confirmed that it is a cross between the American sycamore (*Platanus occidentalis*), brought back in that period from the New World, and the Oriental plane (*P. orientalis*), which is found from Greece to the Himalayas. More robust than its parents, the London plane was extensively planted in France in the 18th century, particularly along canals, partly for use in maintaining the barges and partly to reduce water evaporation. Sadly, the increase in urban pollution has made it vulnerable to canker stain, a fungus disease that has decimated the plane population.

↑ *Platanus x hispanica,* private property.
PROVENCE (FRANCE)

↗ → *Platanus x hispanica,* during and after the bark peeling. NICE (FRANCE)

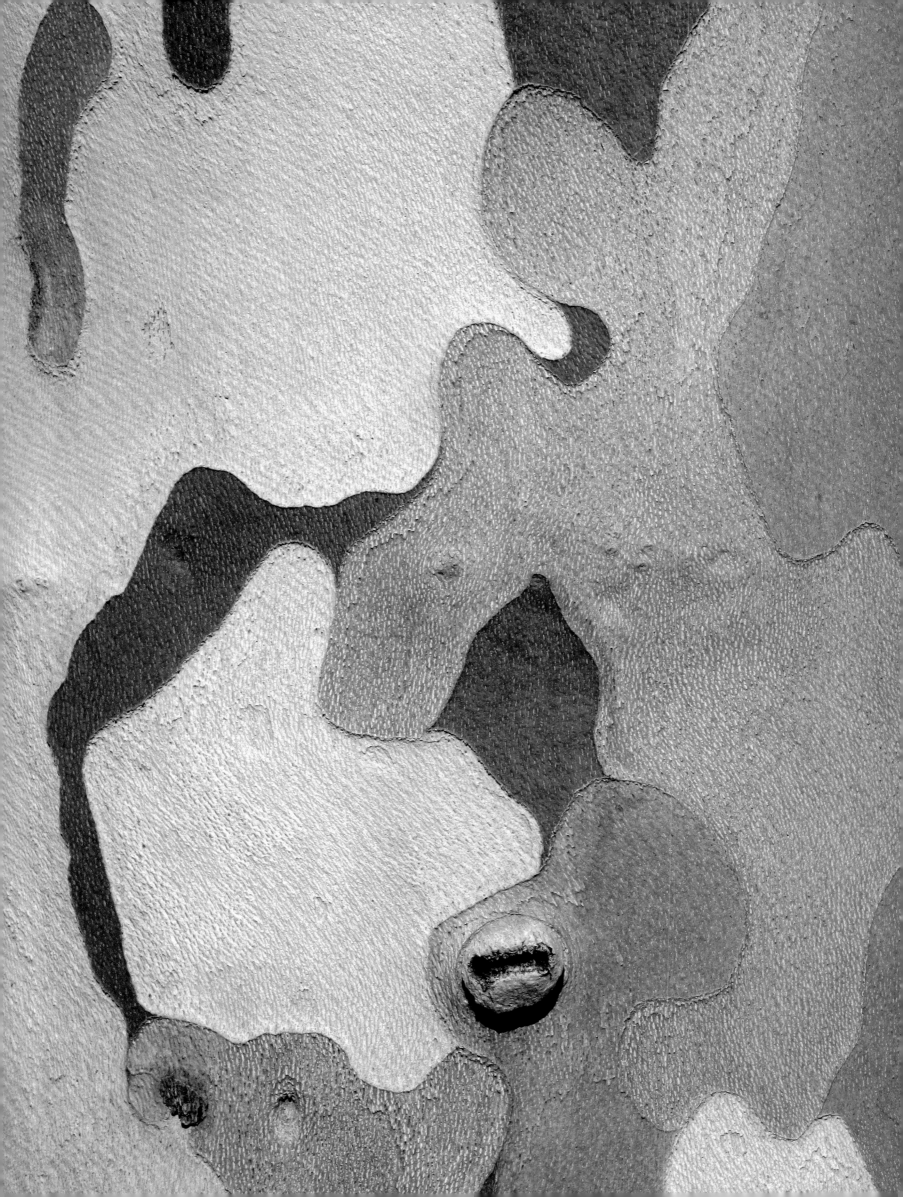

YEW

Taxus baccata

Found throughout Europe, the yew has been under threat of extinction, particularly in the Middle Ages when armies exploited its properties of flexibility and hardness to make bows and other weapons. Although the wood is also highly prized for its attractive reddish grain, the reputation of yew has suffered because all parts of the tree are extremely poisonous, apart from the red flesh of the little fruits (known as arils), each one containing a single seed that is itself highly poisonous. The very slow growth rate of yew has contributed to its decline. In France there are only a few ancient yew plantations left, mainly in Normandy, but with a few rare relics of forests as well, like the one at Saint Baume in Provence. In the last few decades, scientific research into the anti-cancer properties of yew may serve to halt its decline – in the nick of time.

← *Taxus baccata*
WAKEHURST PLACE, ARDINGLY (UK)

→ *Taxus baccata*
JARDIN BOTANIQUE
DE LA VILLE DE LYON (FRANCE)

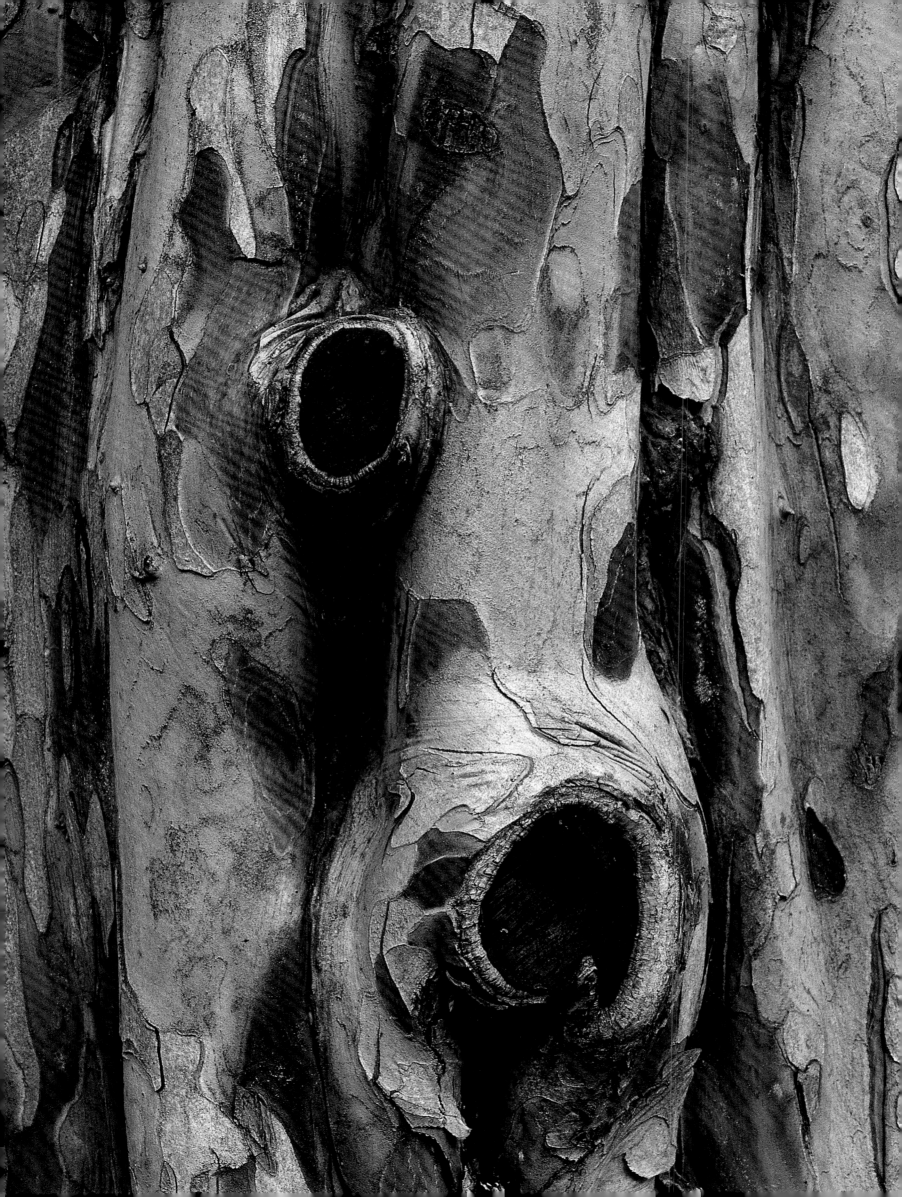

↗ *Populus alba* FRÉJUS (FRANCE)

(SALICACEAE FAMILY)

WHITE POPLAR

Populus alba

The white poplar extends over a huge territory from the southern and central parts of Europe up to the southern part of Siberia and the Himalayas. It is a species that spreads rapidly by suckers, particularly along any watercourse. Copious quantities of seeds are produced, each encased in a little parachute, which enables the seeds to disperse very easily by wind or water. Its foliage, dark green on the upper side, white and downy on the underside, flutters constantly even in the lightest of breezes. The white trunk is covered with lozenge-shaped 'lenticels', little openings in the bark that allow the tree to conduct its essential exchange of gases. Poplars belong to the willow family and their young shoots have been used for centuries. Willow is highly regarded for its healing properties, in particular for the bark from which aspirin is obtained.

↗ *Populus alba* Gattières (France)

↗ *Populus alba*
Arles, Bouches-du-Rhône (France)

↗ *Populus alba*
Fréjus, Var (France)

CHESTNUT

Castanea sativa

The chestnut tree, prized both for food and its healing properties, has been widely planted throughout Europe, from the Caucasus to Portugal, including the southern part of England and Ireland, which makes its actual origins hard to determine. Before becoming a culinary delicacy, the chestnut, nicknamed poor man's bread, had for centuries helped to feed starving peoples in the winter months. The wood, which is very hard, has been used widely both for vine supports and for building materials, such as beams and rafters. The name derives from *Kastana*, the name of towns in both Thessalonika in Greece and the ancient kingdom of Pont in Turkey, each renowned for their chestnut trees. Unfortunately, the spread of fungus diseases like canker and *Phytohthora ramorum* along with the decline in agriculture has seriously reduced the number of chestnut forests.

Castanea sativa, the cracked bark with its twisted fissures. ROYAL BOTANICAL GARDENS KEW, RICHMOND (UK)

OLIVE
Olea europaea

A pillar of European civilization, the olive tree is one of the oldest fruit trees cultivated by man. The first known olives were gathered in Palestine more than 20,000 years ago. And man is first known to have cultivated olives in Jordan and Israel some 2,000 years BC. The Phoenicians and the Romans, both great consumers of olive oil, were responsible for the spread of the olive tree around the Mediterranean. Olive oil has long been used in cooking and for lighting, and also for skin care. A symbol of immortality, and also of peace and friendship, the olive has both oiled the wheels of human relationships and lifted human spirits. Its fruits are enjoyed both as an appetizer and for *tapenades*.

Olea europaea, interior of the trunk. →
OLIVERAIE DE LA COLLE-SUR-LOUP (FRANCE)

↗ *Olea europaea*, spiralling, hollowed trunk. LA COLLE-SUR-LOUP (FRANCE)

A 2,000-year-old olive tree. →
ROQUEBRUNE-CAP-MARTIN (FRANCE)

MARITIME PINE

Pinus pinaster

The maritime pine can be easily recognized from its bark, which has large reddish-purple plates. It grows naturally in the central and western parts of the Mediterranean basin. In 1786 a great replanting of pines was carried out in the Landes region of France to halt the encroachment of the dunes on the villages in that area. It continues to be an important element in reforestation, comprising around 12 per cent of French forests. Since ancient times, the resin has been harvested by cutting notches in its sapwood. A tree will produce an average of 1½ litres (2½ pints) of resin during harvesting. This resin is then boiled or distilled to produce tar or spirit of turpentine, or the block resin that musicians apply to the strings of their bows.

↗ *Pinus pinaster*
Écomusée de la Grande Lande, Sabres (France)

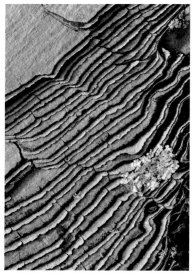

↗ During growth, the layers of bark form strata.

The traditional harvesting of the resin

↗ *Pinus pinaster* Écomusée de la Grande Lande, Sabres (France)

Pinus pinaster →
La Teste de Buch (France)

↗ *Pinus pinea*, hundred-year-old pines maintain their personal space. Jardin botanique de la Villa Thuret, Antibes (France)

UMBRELLA PINE

Pinus pinea

This huge living umbrella more than 30m (100ft) tall is found throughout the northern parts of the Mediterranean basin. Archaeologists have found that homo sapiens was first gathering the cones several thousand years ago. The pine has been cultivated since ancient times, particularly by the Romans who used its wood in carpentry and its seeds (pine kernels) in their cooking, which from then on became a traditional ingredient in Mediterranean cuisine. Spain has become the world-leading producer of this delicacy. The delicate tracery of the umbrella pine's branches creates a huge living puzzle, and also plays its part in offering walkers in summer a unique Mediterranean experience: the scent of pine and the sound of crickets plus the cracking of the cones.

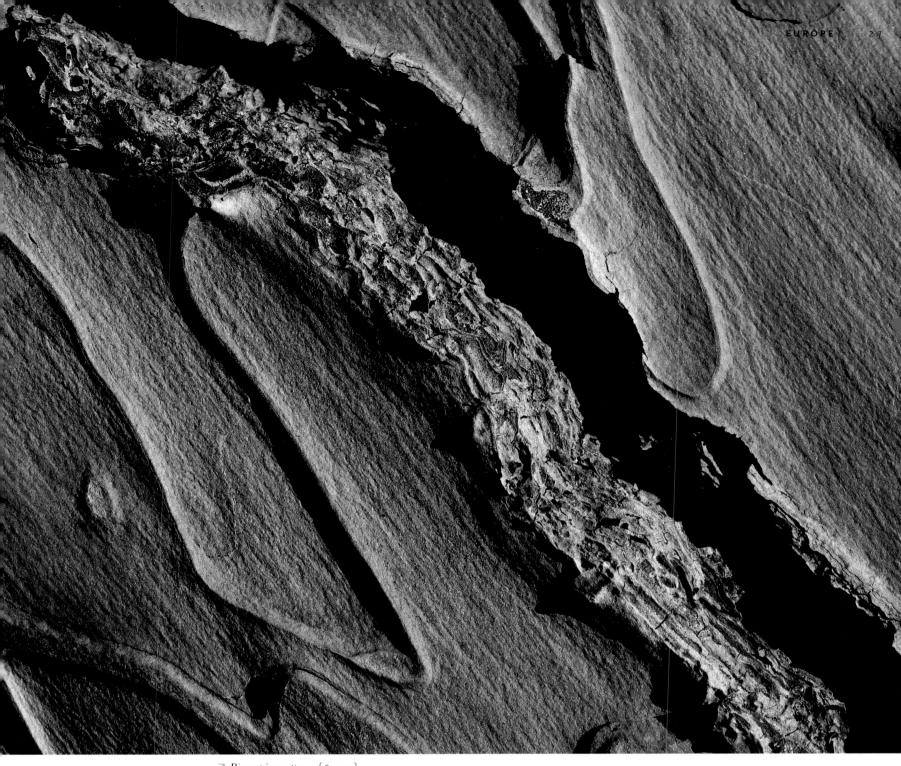

↗ *Pinus pinea* Nice (France)

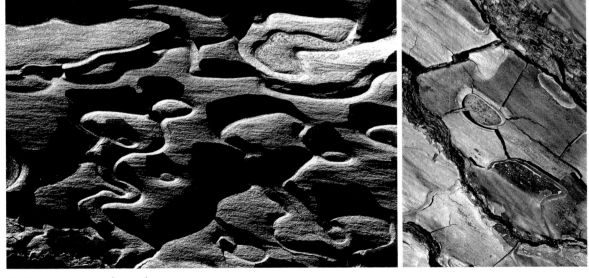

↗ *Pinus pinea* Nice (France).

↗ *Quercus suber* BOIS DE MALVOISIN, PUGET-SUR-ARGENS (FRANCE)

CORK OAK

Quercus suber

A characteristic Mediterranean tree, the cork oak is native to south-west Europe and north-west Africa. Portugal is the uncontested leader in cork production. The use of cork for jar stoppers goes back to more than 500BC. But it was thanks to Dom Perignon, a wine-producing monk in the 17th century, and the inventor of champagne, that the cork acquired its noble credentials. Cork is also valuable as insulation and is used to make cork panels, tiles and suchlike. Its thick bark, which does not burn easily, makes the cork tree a natural barrier in forest fires. Commercial harvesting of the bark takes place every 12 years or so, depending on the customs of the country, and is repeated around 12 times during the life of the tree. New bark has a bright orange hue, which turns a purplish brown and then grey as it ages.

Commercial cork stripping and cork making.

↗ *Quercus suber* ETS PRIMA LIÈGE, FRÉJUS (FRANCE)

Quercus suber →
BOIS DE MALVOISIN
PUGET-SUR-ARGENS (FRANCE)

STRAWBERRY TREE
Arbutus andrachne

The strawberry tree grows mainly in the eastern region of the Mediterranean in Greece and Turkey, and on the shores of the Black Sea. Its soft peeling bark offers a very sensual experience. Its brightest red colours are seen in the spring; then, after the heat of summer, the bark peels progressively in rectangular flakes. Evidence of peeling starts with the outline of rectangles which then begin to separate from the trunk, drying and curling up into little cigar-shaped rolls, revealing the apple-green young bark beneath. Its little red strawberry-like fruits (which have little flavour) have earned the tree its common name. A by-product of the tree is used to cure skin diseases, such as eczema, and it is also used for joint problems, such as arthritis and rheumatism, and to treat gout.

← *Arbutus andrachne*
Jardin botanique de la Villa Thuret,
INRA Antibes (France)

The summer peeling with its fleeting colours.

↗→ *Arbutus andrachne*
Jardin Botanique de la ville de Nice (France)

Strawberry Trees (Madrones)

There are about a dozen species to be found in this genus in Mediterranean climates in southern Europe, the Canary Islands and the western part of North America. The term *Arbutus* comes from a Celtic word, *arbois*, meaning reddish: an allusion to its little bright red fruits, its reddish bark and wood. The European species are known as strawberry trees; the North American ones are called madrone or madrona.

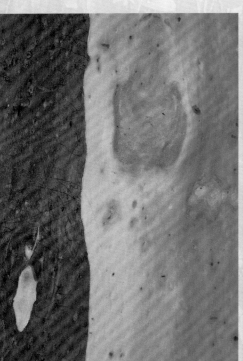   

1. *Arbutus canariensis*
   VILLA THURET, ANTIBES (FRANCE)

2. *Arbutus* x *andrachnoides*
   VILLA THURET, ANTIBES (FRANCE)

3. *Arbutus andrachne*
   JARDIN BOTANIQUE, NICE (FRANCE)

4. *Arbutus andrachne*
   VILLA THURET, ANTIBES (FRANCE)

5. *Arbutus* x *thuretiana*
   VILLA THURET, ANTIBES (FRANCE)

6. *Arbutus* x *thuretiana*
   VILLA THURET, ANTIBES (FRANCE)

7. *Arbutus unedo*
   PARC PHOENIX, NICE (FRANCE)

8. *Arbutus andrachne*
   VILLA THURET, ANTIBES (FRANCE)

9. *Arbutus* x *thuretiana*
   VILLA THURET, ANTIBES (FRANCE)

PAPER BIRCH

Betula papyrifera

North America is covered with great numbers of paper birches, literally the 'tree of life' for the Native American Indians. Its bark, almost indestructible, has an infinite number of uses: being waterproof, it is ideal for canoe making, wigwam roofs, paper and envelopes and torches (it burns easily, even when damp). In spring, the sap can be harvested in the same way as maple syrup. Paper birch water is a well-known cure for gout, cystitis and skin complaints. This special liquid comes in syrup form or can be fermented to make an alcoholic tonic. Its wood is used commercially both in paper manufacturing and as a fuel.

↗ *Betula nigra*
JARDIN DU BOIS MARQUIS, VERNIOZ (FRANCE)

↗ *Betula papyrifera* var. *commutata* WESTONBIRT ARBORETUM, TETBURY (UK)

↗ *Betula alleghaniensis*
ROYAL BOTANIC GARDENS KEW, WAKEHURST PLACE, ARDINGLY (UK)

Betula papyrifera
LES LAURENTIDES, QUÉBEC (CANADA)

↑ *Taxodium distichum*, in its natural milieu. NATIONAL AUDUBON SOCIETY'S CORKSCREW SWAMP SANCTUARY, NAPLES, FLORIDA (USA)

BALD CYPRESS

Taxodium distichum

In autumn, the coppery foliage of the bald cypress sets the damp and dune-studded landscape of the south-eastern states of the USA on fire. It then loses its handsome looks, and in its place you find the bare silhouette, unusual in a conifer, and from which it earns its common name. Also known as the swamp cypress, it is one of those trees, like the mangrove, that demonstrates great tolerance of flooded soil. To fight against conditions that would otherwise suffocate it, it produces curious lung-like protuberances on the trunk, aerial roots of sorts, which are higher than the water level. In the shallow sandy soil, these aerial roots also help to anchor the tree. A bald cyprus can grow up to 1.5m (5ft) tall and they are widely sought after for ship building, as the wood is so hard it never rots.

→
Taxodium distichum,
pleated bark at the level of the first branches.
JARDIN BOTANIQUE DE LA VILLE DE LYON (FRANCE)

STRANGLER FIG

Ficus aurea

Some tropical plants, like lianas and the strangler fig, have a reputation as killers. The strangler fig is a good example. You find it principally in the tropical hardwood forests and in the marshlands of Florida and the Caribbean. Spread by birds, its seeds lodge and germinate high up in the joints between the trunk and branch of a tree or between the palm frond and trunk of a palm tree. The ensuing young fig tree begins life as an epiphyte before the roots twine around the trunk of the host tree until they reach the ground, at which point they begin to suffocate the host tree. Deprived of essential light, the host tree that provided the support starts to die. In the end it can disappear, so the roots of the fig form a kind of living tower around what was formerly the host.

← *Ficus aurea*
MOUNTS BOTANICAL GARDEN,
WEST PALM BEACH, FLORIDA (USA)

→ *Ficus aurea*
MIAMI, FLORIDA (USA)

↗ A young *Ficus aurea* on a cabbage palm. EVERGLADES NATIONAL PARK, FLORIDA (USA)

↗ An older *Ficus aurea* on a gumbo limbo. MONTGOMERY BOTANICAL CENTER, CORAL GABLES, FLORIDA (USA)

GUMBO LIMBO

Bursera simaruba

This tree grows from Mexico to the northernmost tropical parts of southern USA, but also in Florida and the Caribbean. You see it a lot in coastal regions as it tolerates salt winds well and can even cope with the violent storms created by cyclones. It is sometimes nicknamed the tourist tree because its reddish bark peels off like that of a sunburnt tourist! Like the incense (*Boswellia*) and myrrh (*Commiphora*) trees that it is closely related to, it produces a gum or resin that the natives use for medicines, incense, glue and varnish. Its bark is thought to be an antidote to the poisonous sap of the Florida poison tree (*Metopium toxiferum*). The seeds, covered in their fleshy red fruits, are a great attraction for many kinds of bird, which then help to spread the seeds.

↗ *Bursera simaruba*
Fairchild Tropical Botanic Garden, Coral, Gables, Florida (USA)

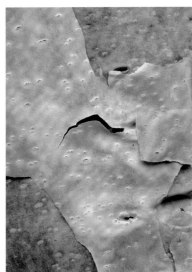

↗ *Bursera microphylla*
Moorten Botanical Gardens, Palm Springs, California (USA)

←
→ *Bursera simaruba*
Montgomery Botanical Center, Coral Gables, Florida (USA)

CABBAGE PALM

Sabal palmetto

The cabbage palm is emblematic of the Florida and South Carolina coastline, where it is found among the marshes. It tolerates a wide range of taxing conditions: salty, humid, dry and very cold. To these horticultural benefits you can add its beautiful foliage and interesting trunk. The base of the palm fronds forms a kind of living corset that can remain for years, depending on the tree in question. Over time, debris accumulates in the pockets and allows all kind of ferns, orchids and other epiphytes to lodge there, including the strangler fig. Its young buds are edible (heart of palm), but cutting them off kills the tree. The palm fronds themselves are used in many different crafts, including hat, basket and rope making and excellent honey is produced from its nectar-rich flowers.

↑ *Sabal palmetto* with its feet in the water in its natural habitat. Everglades National Park, Florida (USA)

↗ *Sabal palmetto*
differing trunk colours of individual specimens.
Everglades National Park, Florida (USA)

↗ *Sabal mauritiiformis*
Montgomery Botanical Center,
Coral Gables, Florida (USA)

ROYAL PALM

Roystonea regia

This tall, elegant palm, with its supple trunk, is characteristic of Cuba's landscape. It is extremely useful for the native population, who exploit every part of it. A bottle-shaped tree, it is characteristically bulbous at the base and part way up the trunk, which makes it easy to distinguish from other species. In young specimens, the bark has rings of colour that range from deep chestnut to light green near the base of its palm fronds. The common name pays homage to the American general, Roy Stone, who fought for the annexation of Puerto Rico during the Spanish-American war and demonstrated his love for Cuba by participating in its development by helping to safeguard the islanders and improving the road network. Cuba is also home to another species of royal palm (*R. borinquena*).

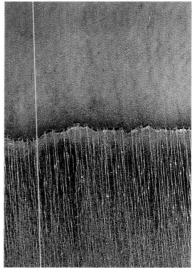

↗→ *Roystonea regia*
Nouméa (New Caledonia)

← *Roystonea regia*
Montgomery Botanical Center,
Coral Gables, Florida (USA)

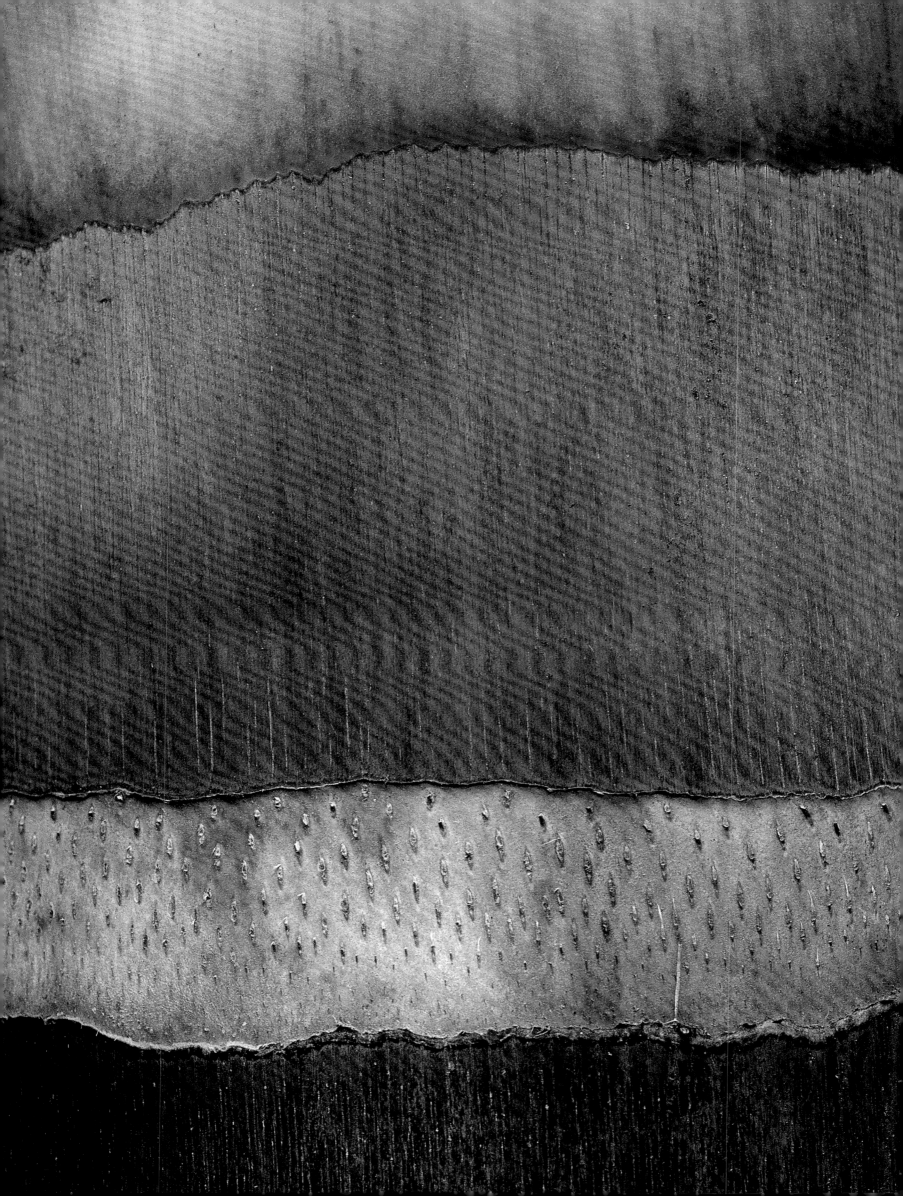

Palm trees

There are nearly 3,000 different species of palm, which originate in the tropical regions of the world. Despite their sometimes massive stature (more than 60m/200ft tall and more than 5m/16ft in girth for the most imposing of them), some are categorized as giant perennials rather than trees. They produce neither wood nor growth rings. Man has made use of all parts of these plants to feed, shelter and clothe himself, and also to make various craft artefacts.

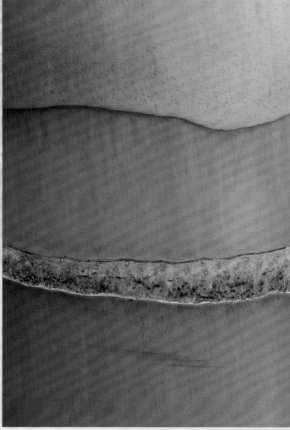

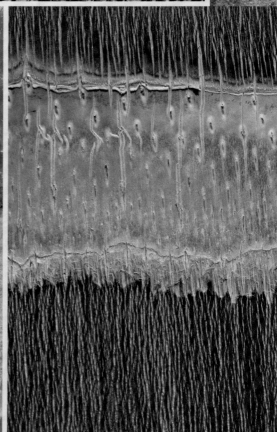

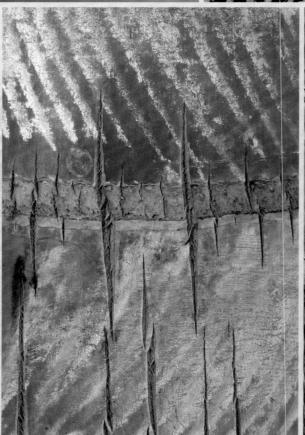

1. *Trithrinax campestris*
   St-Aygulf (France)

2. *Carpoxylon macrospermum*
   Fairchild, Coral Gables (USA)

3. *Coccothrinax miraguama*
   Montgomery, Coral Gables (USA)

4. *Clinostigma harlandii*
   Fairchild, Coral Gables (USA)

5. *Roystonea regia*
   Montgomery, Coral Gables (USA)

6. *Jubaea chilensis*
   Villa Thuret, Antibes (France)

7. *Livistona drudei*
   Kew Gardens, Richmond (UK)

8. *Metroxylon sagu*
   Kebun Raya Bogor (Indonesia)

9. *Washingtonia robusta*
   Nice (France)

10. *Butia capitata*
    Canet-en-Roussillon (France)

11. *Hyophorbe verschaffeltii*
    Kebun Raya Cibodas (Indonesia)

12. *Dypsis decaryi*
    Ranomafana (Madagascar)

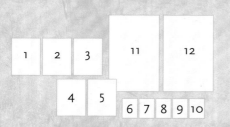

MADRONE

Arbutus menziesii

In 1790 the Scottish naturalist Archibald Menzies was appointed as naturalist to accompany Captain George Vancouver on his voyage around the world on HMS Discovery, during which he discovered this monumental tree on the west coast of North America. Its supple orange-red bark peels off during the summer, revealing the new apple-green bark beneath. The Native American Indians used the bark for tanning hides. They also believed it had a number of medicinal properties. Its wood makes excellent charcoal, which in turn was used to make gunpowder. The madrone is a pyrophite – a plant that both resists fire and uses it to propagate itself. After scorching, the seeds germinate more easily as other competitors for light are eliminated. The tree regenerates itself very quickly and the new shoots grow from the old stumps. Sadly, the improved control of forest fires has reduced the madrone's ability to regenerate itself.

↗ *Arbutus menziesii* at the start of peeling

→
← *Arbutus menziesii*
UNIVERSITY OF CALIFORNIA, BOTANICAL
GARDEN, BERKELEY, CALIFORNIA (USA)

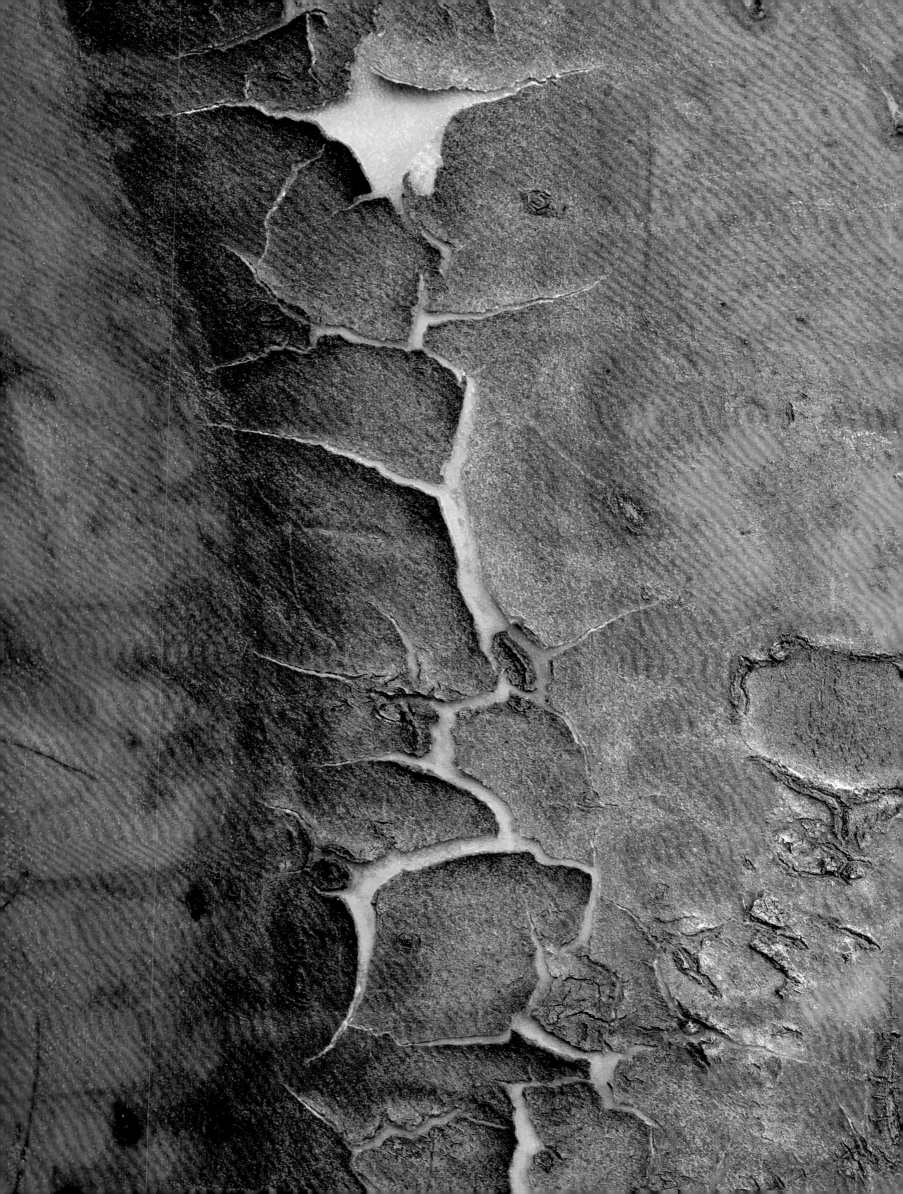

↑ A coastal forest of 1000-year-old *Sequoia sempervirens*. MUIR WOODS NATIONAL MONUMENT, CALIFORNIA (USA)

COAST REDWOOD

Sequoia sempervirens

In contrast to the giant redwood (*Sequoiadendron giganteum*), which is found well inland, the coast redwood inhabits the Californian coast, from south of Monterey to south of Oregon. It benefits from the sea mists to get its necessary uptake of water. It has the record for the tallest tree in the world (115m/380ft) and has one of the thickest, most fibrous barks, a natural protection against fire. The oldest trees have no branches for tens of metres up their lower trunks, thereby limiting possible fire damage. The bark and the wood are cinnamon-coloured, indicating the presence of tannins which help to protect the tree from fungus and bacterial diseases. For all these reasons, the redwood is a greatly venerated tree. Its Latin name pays homage to the Cherokee Indian, Sequoyah.

↗
Sequoia sempervirens, the undulating bark of some
specimens many hundreds of years old.
MUIR WOODS NATIONAL MONUMENT, CALIFORNIA (USA)

SERPENTINE MANZANITA

Arctostaphylos obispoensis

There are nearly 60 species of manzanita, all originating in the western parts of North America, from the south of British Colombia to central Mexico. Its name comes from the Greek arkto, meaning 'bear', and *staphyle*, meaning 'grape', as its little fruits (bearberries) are very much appreciated by bears. The common name, manzanita, is Spanish for 'little apple'. This ornamental shrub grows naturally in the San Luis Obispo region of California. Its greyish-green foliage contrasts beautifully with its thin reddish-purple bark. It starts to peel at the beginning of summer, and progressively reveals green, orange, reddish-brown and purple colours. Just like its close relative the arbutus, manzanita is used to cure urinary infections, thanks to a substance called arbutine, a glycoside contained by the bearberries.

←
→ *Arctostaphylos obispoensis*
UNIVERSITY OF CALIFORNIA, BOTANICAL
GARDEN, BERKELEY, CALIFORNIA (USA)

SMOOTH ARIZONA CYPRESS

Cupressus glabra

The smooth cypress is a hardy species discovered in the 20th century in the Green River Canyon in Arizona. Some experts think it is a variety of Cupressus arizonica (the Arizona cypress); others consider it to be a completely different species. Nevertheless, it differs from it owing to the presence of resin glands on its aromatic, blue-grey foliage, its very hard wood and its very distinctive bark – the tree trunk is multicoloured, the top layer peeling into flakes, leaving the underlying bark very smooth, hence its Latin name, glabra, meaning 'smooth'. When planted in rows, it makes a very good windbreak and an impenetrable hedge. Thanks to its ability to withstand drought, it is a popular ornamental plant in the south of France.

←↗ *Cupressus glabra,* the diversity of bark colours. FRÉJUS (FRANCE)

→

Cupressus glabra, resin markings that appear after peeling. FRÉJUS (FRANCE)

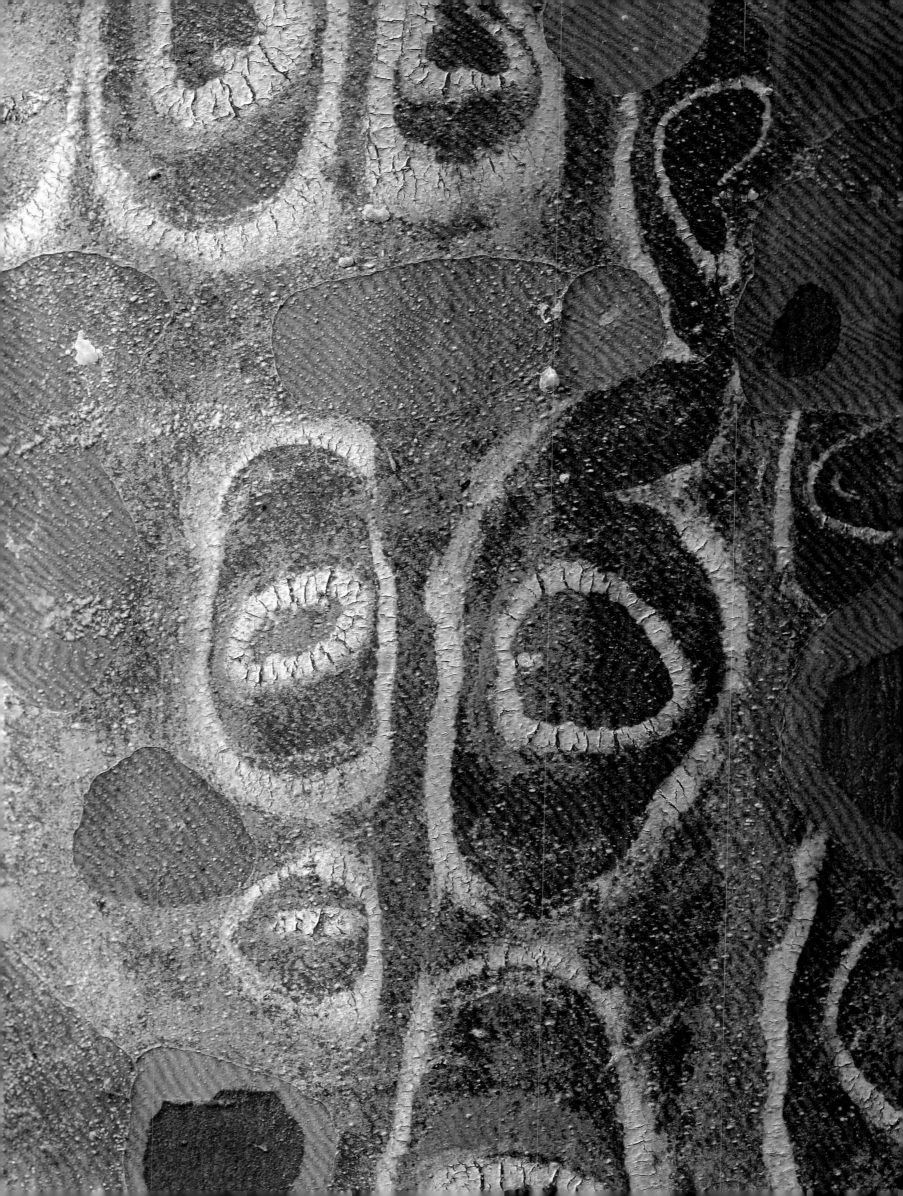

↗ *Pinus longaeva*, 'The Patriarch', with its colossal trunk more than 11m (36ft) in circumference. ANCIENT BRISTLECONE PINE FOREST, THE PATRIARCH GROVE CALIFORNIA (USA)

[PINACEAE FAMILY]

BRISTLECONE PINE

Pinus longaeva

The bristlecone pine, named for the numbers of tiny spines on the scales of its fruits, is one of the oldest life forms in the world. The oldest known specimen, nicknamed 'Methuselah', is more than 4,700 years old. Their twisted silhouettes and bare branches define the ghostly landscape of the White Mountains of California. There, the 3,000m (10,000ft) altitude and long, hard winters contrast with the burning dry summer heat of the toughest of deserts. It owes its amazing longevity to its very hard living conditions. In order to survive, it has to stop its growth, keeping its needles for decades before renewing them and managing to survive with just a few branches covered in bark, which keeps it alive.

↗ *Pinus longaeva*, with its naturally peeled trunk.
ANCIENT BRISTLECONE PINE FOREST, THE PATRIARCH GROVE CALIFORNIA (USA)

↗ *Pinus longaeva* ANCIENT BRISTLECONE PINE FOREST, SCHULMAN GROVE, CALIFORNIA (USA)

Pines

Pines are the most varied of all conifers, in which the bark peels into different colours and shapes. There are more than 100 species which have spontaneously developed in the northern hemisphere, principally from California to Mexico, but you also find them planted all over the southern hemisphere too. They are used for their wood, their resin and sometimes for their edible pine nuts. Some species of pine (*P. longaeva*), being thousands of years old, are among the oldest living species of all kinds.

1. *Pinus pinaster*
   GÉNÉRARGUES (FRANCE)

2. *Pinus strobus*
   KEW GARDENS,
   RICHMOND (UK)

3. *Pinus ponderosa*
   SIERRA NEVADA,
   CALIFORNIA (USA)

4. *Pinus pinea*
   NICE (FRANCE)

5. *Pinus laricio*
   CORSE (FRANCE)

6. *Pinus densiflora*
   HILLIER GARDENS,
   AMPFIELD (UK)

7. *Pinus halepensis*
   ST-JEAN-CAP-FERRAT
   (FRANCE)

8. *Pinus sylvestris*
   LA MARTRE (FRANCE)

9. *Pinus wallichiana*
   WAKEHURST PLACE,
   ARDINGLY (UK)

10. *Pinus jeffreyi*
    SIERRA NEVADA,
    CALIFORNIA (USA)

11. *Pinus bungeana*
    JARDIN BOTANIQUE
    DE LYON (FRANCE)

12. *Pinus contorta*
    SIERRA NEVADA,
    CALIFORNIA (USA)

BLUE PALOVERDE

Parkinsonia florida

The genus *Parkinsonia,* taking its name from John Parkinson, the renowned 17th century English botanist, comprises a dozen species from the semi-arid regions of Africa and America. The majority of American species are called *paloverde* (literally 'green branch' in Spanish), alluding to the colour of their bark. In high temperatures, the tiny blue-green leaves fall, leaving the bark to do the necessary work of photosynthesis. In spring, with its pendant branches, it makes a spectacular golden ball which illuminates the desert landscapes from the south-west of the States down to the north of Mexico. Its seeds are edible: eaten fresh, they taste like peas; dried and crushed, they were used for flour by Native American Indians.

← *Parkinsonia florida*
PALM DESERT, CALIFORNIA (USA)

→ *Parkinsonia florida,* as it ages the bark loses its ability to photosynthesize. THE LIVING DESERT, PALM DESERT, CALIFORNIA (USA)

OCOTILLO

Fouquieria splendens

At first glance the ocotillo looks like a spiny shrub, showing few signs of life. On closer inspection, you can see the bark is torn in long, vertical strips, revealing yellowish-green photosynthetic tissue that takes over during leaf fall in the dry season. The best specimens can reach 10m (33ft) in height and can have as many as 50 or more branches. The spiny shoots are useful for fence posts and root easily, creating a great thorny hedge. In the spring, large quantities of nectar-rich red flowers decorate the desert from the south-west of the States to the north of Mexico. The ocotillo is a medicinal plant that was used by the Native Americans. Its Latin name comes from Pierre Eloi Fouquier, the physician to two kings of France, Charles X and Louis Philippe Iˢᵗ.

←
→ *Fouquieria splendens*
JOSHUA TREE NATIONAL PARK, CALIFORNIA (USA)

↗ *Washingtonia robusta* Malaga (Spain)

MEXICAN WASHINGTONIA

Washingtonia robusta

Cultivated throughout the subtropical regions of the world, Mexican Washingtonia is a tall palm, originating in the canyons and valleys from Lower California to Mexico. With its head in the sun and its feet in water, it can grow quickly to more than 30m (100ft) tall. The American species (*W. filifera*) is a tougher, stockier plant. In its natural state, you will find it clothed with a protective skirt of old, dried palm fronds that are still attached to the trunk. Once cut, the petioles form a decorative latticework. With more radical cutting, and the loss of its restraining corset, the trunk becomes more and more reddish the closer it gets to the crown. The Latin name of the genus pays homage to George Washington, hero of the American War of Independence and the first President of the United States of America.

↗ *Washingtonia robusta,* covered with fibres from the base to the crown. Nice (France)

↗ *Washingtonia filifera* in its natural habitat. Palm Canyon, California (USA)

↗ *Washingtonia robusta* Nice (France)

MEXICAN GRASS TREE

Nolina longifolia

This elegant grass tree, a close cousin of the yucca, thrives in the tropical climate of central and southern Mexico, particularly in the Oaxaca region. It copes very well with the cold. In France, specimens more than a hundred years old can be found in the gardens of the Cote d'Azur having successfully survived some hard winters. It has distinctive long, fine, drooping leaves more than 2m (6ft) long, as the Latin name longifolia or 'long-leaf' suggests. Flexible and easy to plait, the leaves are used both for baskets and for thatching traditional Mexican buildings. The grass tree has a characteristic, cork-like bark, with deep fissures, and a short trunk. There are more than 30 species in the genus, taking the name of the French agronomist and horticultural writer, P.C. Nolin.

↑
→
Nolina longifolia
with its deeply fissured bark.
Serre de la Madone, Menton (France)

BULL'S HORN ACACIA

Acacia sphaerocephala (syn. *Vachellia sphaerostachya*)

The genus *Acacia* contains about 1,350 species scattered throughout the sub-tropical regions of the world, principally in Africa and Australia. Recently some specialists have classified the uniquely Australian species as Acacia. Those from other continents have been given the synonym *Vachellia sphaerostachya*. However, many have continued to call all the species by the generic name of Acacia. The foliage is a useful source of nourishment for animals, and some species have developed strategies to resist their depradations, as is the case with this acacia originating in central America. It lives in perfect symbiosis with colonies of ants *(Pseudomyrmex ferruginea)*. Neither can do without the other. The tree offers the ants both shelter and food. The great hypertrophic spines on the trunk provide the ants (who bore holes in them) with a home, while the leaves, exuding a nectar high in oils and proteins, provide the ants with essential nutrients. These are known as Beltian bodies (after Thomas Belt, a 19th century naturalist who studied the plant). For their part, the ants protect the tree by scenting any likely aggressors and attacking them.

←
→ *Acacia sphaerocephala*
St-Jean-Cap-Ferrat (France)

↗ *Acacia xanthophloea*
Kruger National Park
(South Africa)

↗ *Acacia cyperophylla* var. *cyperophylla*
Gascoyne River, Western Australia
(Australia)

↗ *Acacia karoo*
Parc Phoenix, Nice
(France)

↗ *Acacia origena*
Hajara
(Yemen)

↗ Psidium guajava
JARDÍN BOTÁNICO-HISTÓRICO LA CONCEPCIÓN, MALAGA (SPAIN)

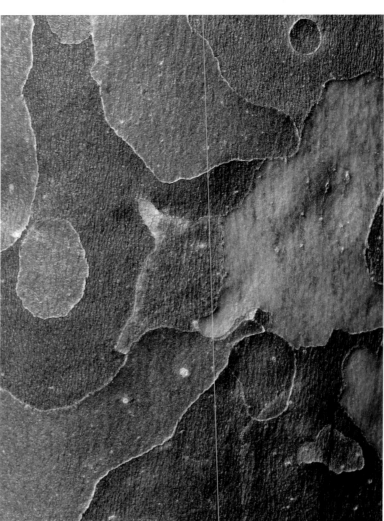

↗ Psidium guineense
PARC PHOENIX, NICE (FRANCE)

↗ Psidium guajava
JARDÍN BOTÁNICO-HISTÓRICO LA CONCEPCIÓN,
MALAGA (SPAIN)

COMMON GUAVA
Psidium guajava

The guava is a small tree from the regions of southern Mexico and central America which is widely cultivated throughout the tropics; it is often invasive in its habitat. Rich in vitamins and trace elements, the fruit is eaten fresh or made into jams and jellies. All parts of the guava tree have medicinal properties: the leaves are thought to be good for diabetes, diarrhoea and gastrointestinal problems and even to fight cancer. The bark, which is rich in tannins, is used in central America to tan hides while the aromatic leaves are used as a dyestuff for textiles in South-East Asia.

PAPAYA

Carica papaya

The papaya, growing from southern Mexico to the northern part of South America, is widely grown through the tropics. The papaya fruit, rich in vitamins, can be eaten green as a vegetable or when ripe as a fruit. The green fruit is rich in papain, an enzyme that is used to tenderize meat. The American Indians made use of this unique property for centuries, wrapping their meat in papaya leaves before cooking it. Papain is beneficial to the digestion, helps to heal wounds and is good for the nervous system. The seeds can be ground to replace pepper.

←↗ *Carica papaya,* the natural scars that form after the leaves fall. AMBOSITRA (MADAGASCAR).

Cauliflory

The flowers of woody plants generally appear on the current year's growth or on young leafy branches. Cauliflory (from the Latin *caulis* 'stem' and *flos* 'flower') is a condition found in trees and woody vines where flowers and fruit are borne directly on the trunks and older branches, which facilitates cross-pollination and therefore the dissemination of the seed. You will find this particular tropical phenomenon in more than a hundred plants, the best known of which are the cacao plant (*Theobroma*), the calabash (*Crescentia*) or the breadfruit (*Artocarpus*).

1. *Phyllarthron* sp.
   FORÊT DE KIRINDY
   (MADAGASCAR)

2. *Cercis siliquastrum*
   PARC PHOENIX, NICE
   (FRANCE)

3. *Saraca palembanica*
   KEBUN RAYA BOGOR
   (INDONESIA)

4. *Parmentiera cerifera*
   KEBUN RAYA BOGOR
   (INDONESIA)

5. *Ficus racemosa*
   MONTGOMERY, CORAL
   GABLES (USA)

6. *Averrhoa bilimbi*
   GIFFORD ARBORETUM,
   UNIVERSITY OF MIAMI
   (USA)

7. *Diospyros cauliflora*
   KEBUN RAYA BOGOR
   (INDONESIA)

8. *Ceratonia siliqua*
   NICE (FRANCE)

9. *Ficus heteropoda*
   KEBUN RAYA BOGOR
   (INDONESIA)

10. *Theobroma cacao*
    CIOMAS BOGOR
    (INDONESIA)

11. *Artocarpus heterophyllus*
    RUMPIN (INDONESIA)

12. *Crescentia cujete*
    FRUIT AND SPICE PARK,
    HOMESTEAD (USA)

SHAVING BRUSH TREE
Pseudobombax ellipticum

Originating in the south of Mexico, Guatemala, Salvador and Honduras, the delicate flowers of the shaving brush tree adorn the gardens and churches of the tropical regions of the American continent, where it has naturalized. The flowers, either red or white according to the variety, appear in the winter after the leaves have fallen. The common name derives from its big stamens, more than 10cm (4in) long, which resemble a shaving brush. In Salvador the flowers are used to make a tisane to alleviate stomach upsets. Like the kapok tree, it belongs to the *Bombacaceae* family in which the characteristic fruits are filled with silky fibres that are used to fill pillows and mattresses, and to insulate fridges. The wood, which is easy to work, is used for a wide range of local artefacts.

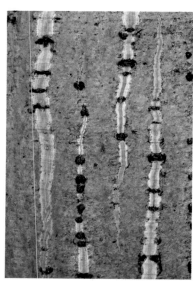

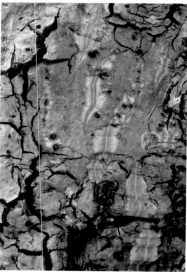

← ↗ *Pseudobombax ellipticum*
MONTGOMERY BOTANICAL CENTER,
CORAL GABLES, FLORIDA (USA)

→
Pseudobombax ellipticum
a scaly motif on the base of the trunk.
ETS KUENTZ, FRÉJUS (FRANCE)

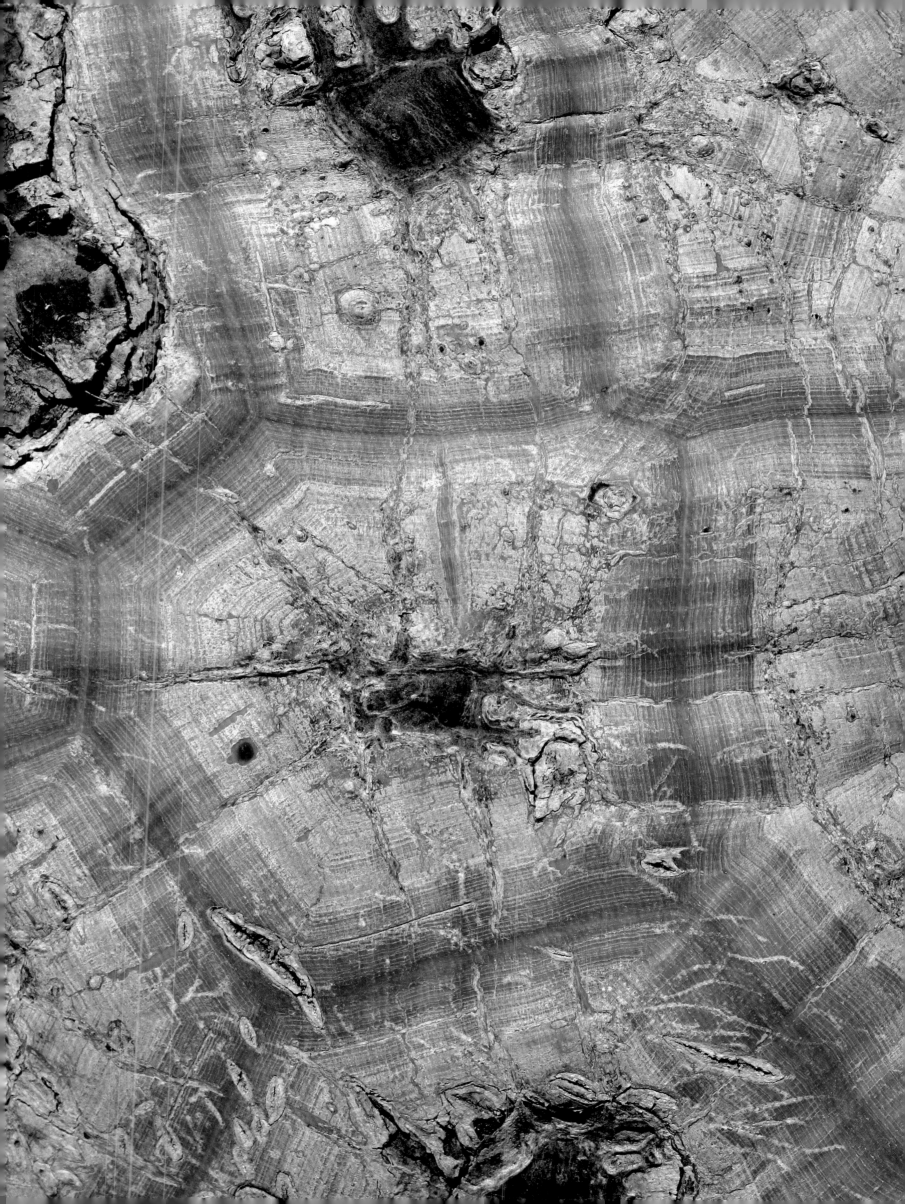

KAPOK TREE

Ceiba pentandra

Many species of *Ceiba* (the Latin name also given recently to all the *Chorisia* genus) have green bark studded with spines. The most majestic of all of them is the kapok tree. For the Maya people, it was considered sacred, the connecting link between the subterranean, earthly and heavenly kingdoms. Native to the Caribbean and to central and southern America, it has been planted throughout the tropical areas of the world. It is a medicinal tree that can cure a wide range of complaints. Its banana-shaped fruit contains a light, waterproof, insulating and indestructible fibre called kapok. It is used for mattresses, lifejackets and for thermal insulation. The saponin in its seeds is a natural form of soap. The name *Ceiba* was given to this revered tree by the Tainos, an ancient Native American tribe from the Greater Antilles. It has become the symbol of both Puerto Rico and Guatemala.

↗ *Ceiba aesculifolia*
MONTGOMERY BOTANICAL CENTER,
CORAL GABLES, FLORIDA (USA)

↗ *Ceiba insignis*, bottle-like trunk.
JARDIN EXOTIUQE DE MONACO

←
→ *Ceiba pentandra*, and its huge spines.
KEBUN RAYA BOGOR, WEST JAWA (INDONESIA)

TREE OF LIFE
Guaiacum officinale

This little tree hails from the coastal areas of the Gulf of Mexico and the Caribbean. Its precious black wood is one of the heaviest in the world. It is used to make mortarboards, mallets and the gavels used in the Courts of Justice. It has long been used in boatbuilding for making pulleys as it combines the qualities of durability and lubrication (a useful antidote to chafing ropes). Sadly, it is now on the way to becoming extinct in the Caribbean islands. Its Latin name *officinale* indicates that it is a plant originally used in pharmacy. It was introduced into Europe by the Spanish at the beginning of the 16th century under the name of *Palo sancta* (holy tree) or *Lignum vitae* (tree of life). Although all of the tree has medicinal properties, it is the heartwood that has mostly been used to treat syphilis, gout, rheumatic disorders and skin conditions.

← *Guaiacum officinale*
Montgomery Botanical Center,
Coral Gables, Florida (USA)

→
Guaiacum officinale
Fairchild Topical Botanic Garden,
Coral Gables, Florida (USA)

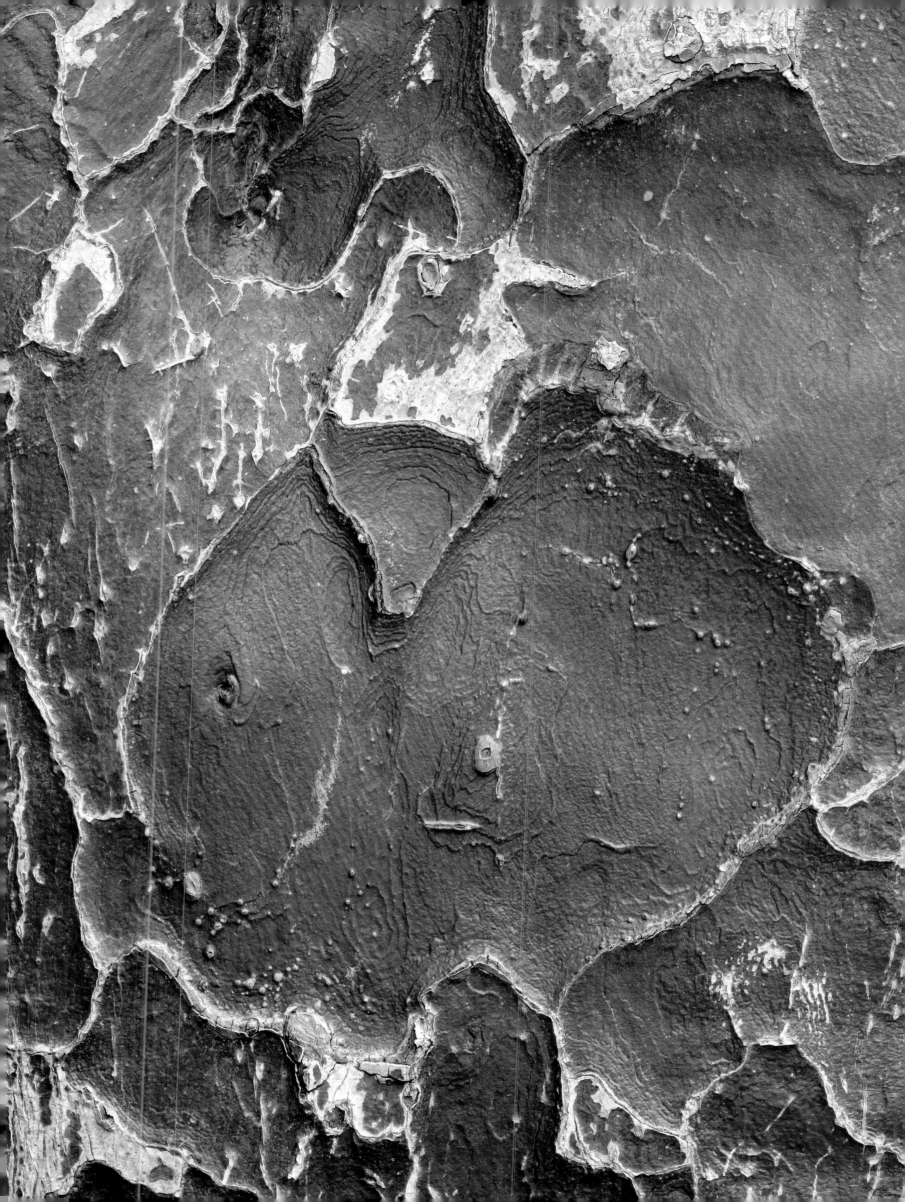

↗ Tapping a plantation of *Hevea brasiliensis* in the early morning. Rumpin, West Java (Indonesia)

RUBBER TREE

Hevea brasiliensis

Far from their origins in the Amazon, rubber trees, the major supplier of natural latex, have been cultivated mainly since the end of the 19th century in South-East Asia. Latex is in fact found in almost 7,500 other species of plant. Pre-Colombian civilizations used it in their ball games, the probable precursor of the modern game of basketball. When it is five years old, the Rubber Tree's inside layer of bark is tapped for its rich reserves of latex. A rubber tree can produce 5kg (12lb) of rubber a year for a lifetime of around 25 to 30 years. This basic product, by virtue of its elasticity and suppleness, has revolutionized transport and our daily lives. Natural rubber remains competitive with its artificial counterparts, particularly for vehicle tyres, surgical gloves and condoms.

↗ *Hevea brasiliensis* with the rubber flowing after being tapped.

Natural rubber: traditional harvesting of latex from the rubber tree

↗ *Hevea brasiliensis* Rumpin, West Java (Indonesia)

TABAQUILLO

Polylepis australis

Well above the limit of the traditional tree line, these little trees with their twisted trunks are found on the slopes of Cordoba Mountains in the Andes. They have the world record for flowering plants at high altitude (more than 5,200m/1,7000ft for the species P. tarapacana in Bolivia). The name polyepis means 'squamous' or 'scale-like', referring to its bark which is covered in scales that protect it from extreme cold on the one hand and forest fires on the other. The tabaquillo (literally, 'little tobacco') gets its name from the use of its bark as cigarette papers by the Native American Indians. It is the most southerly species (hence the name australis). You can find it at altitudes of up to 3,500m (12,000ft) in the northern and central parts of Argentina. The forests of Polyepis are among the most threatened in the world, owing to intensive farming on the one hand and frequent forest fires on the other, which prevent its natural regeneration.

←
→ *Polylepis australis*
ROYAL BOTANIC GARDENS KEW,
WAKEHURST PLACE, ARDINGLY (UK)

CHILEAN MYRTLE

Myrtus luma

The Chilean myrtle is a small, slow-growing tree but can reach up to 20m (65ft) in height in its natural habitat – the tropical/temperate belt around Valdivian, in the centre of the Sierra de Cordoba in the Andes. The name *luma* comes from the word kelumamull (orange wood), the common name for the tree used by the indigenous Mapuche people. Like the common myrtle (*Myrtus communis*), it has aromatic leaves that are used medicinally. The nectar of the fragrant white flowers contributes to a woodland honey that is much appreciated in Chile, as are its sweet, edible fruits. Like a great number of the *Myrtaceae* family, the adult trees develop an interesting bark. Rounded portions of bark peel off, leaving behind white blotches on the fine, reddish, parchment-like bark beneath.

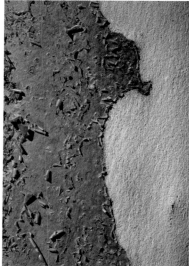

↗ *Myrtus luma*
SIR HAROLD HILLIER GARDENS,
AMPFIELD (UK)

←
→ *Myrtus luma*
SIR HAROLD HILLIER GARDENS,
AMPFIELD (UK)

Eucalyptus regnans, the king of the eucalyptuses, can reach nearly 100m (330ft) in height, STYX VALLEY BIG TREE RESERVE, TASMANIA (AUSTRALIA)

BLACK TREE FERN
Cyathea medullaris

Tree ferns develop a false trunk that can reach nearly 30m (100ft) in height in the biggest specimens. You can count up to 1,000 species grouped into two main genera: *Cyathea* and *Dicksonia*. They are associated most frequently with hot, humid tropical climates. However, some species, originating in the Australian continent, are frost-resistant. That is true of this little native black tree fern, found in New Zealand, Fiji and the Polynesian islands. Its blue-black trunk is covered with oval scars, left behind when the old fronds fall. Unlike flowering plants, ferns produce spores. The genus name Cyathea comes from the Greek kyatheion meaning 'little dish', recalling the form of the little envelopes holding the spores under the leaves.

↗ *Cyathea intermedia*
PLACE DES COCOTIERS,
NOUMÉA (NEW CALEDONIA)

↗ *Cyathea cooperi*
PARC PHOENIX, NICE
(FRANCE)

←
→ *Cyathea medullaris,* scars that appear when the fern fronds fall.
KERIKERI (NEW ZEALAND)

NEW ZEALAND KAORI

Agathis australis

The genus *Agathis* is a primitive tropical conifer that first appeared in the Eocene period several million years ago. The New Zealand kaori is the sacred tree of the Maoris. It is highly regarded for its light, supple, precious and indestructible wood. The flammable resin serves for heating, lighting, varnishes and even for jewellery. A powder obtained from its ashes was used as a black pigment in tattooing. In the 19th century, the colonial powers over-exploited this natural resource and today there are only a few small protected forests left. A few ancient specimens, thousands of years old, can be found in the Coromandel Peninsula and on North Island at the Waipoua Forest Sanctuary. From its imposing height of 51m (170ft) and its impressive girth of more than 14m (45ft), the king of the forest or '*Tane Mahuta*', as it is known in Maori, keeps watch over a sanctuary of the kaori trees.

↗ WAIPOUA FOREST SANCTUARY (NEW ZEALAND)

← The best-known *Agathis astralis* in North Island, New Zealand.
WAIPOUA FOREST SANCTUARY (NEW ZEALAND)

→
Losing bark regularly helps *Agathis australis* to get rid of any epiphytes. WAIPOUA FOREST SANCTUARY
(NEW ZEALAND)

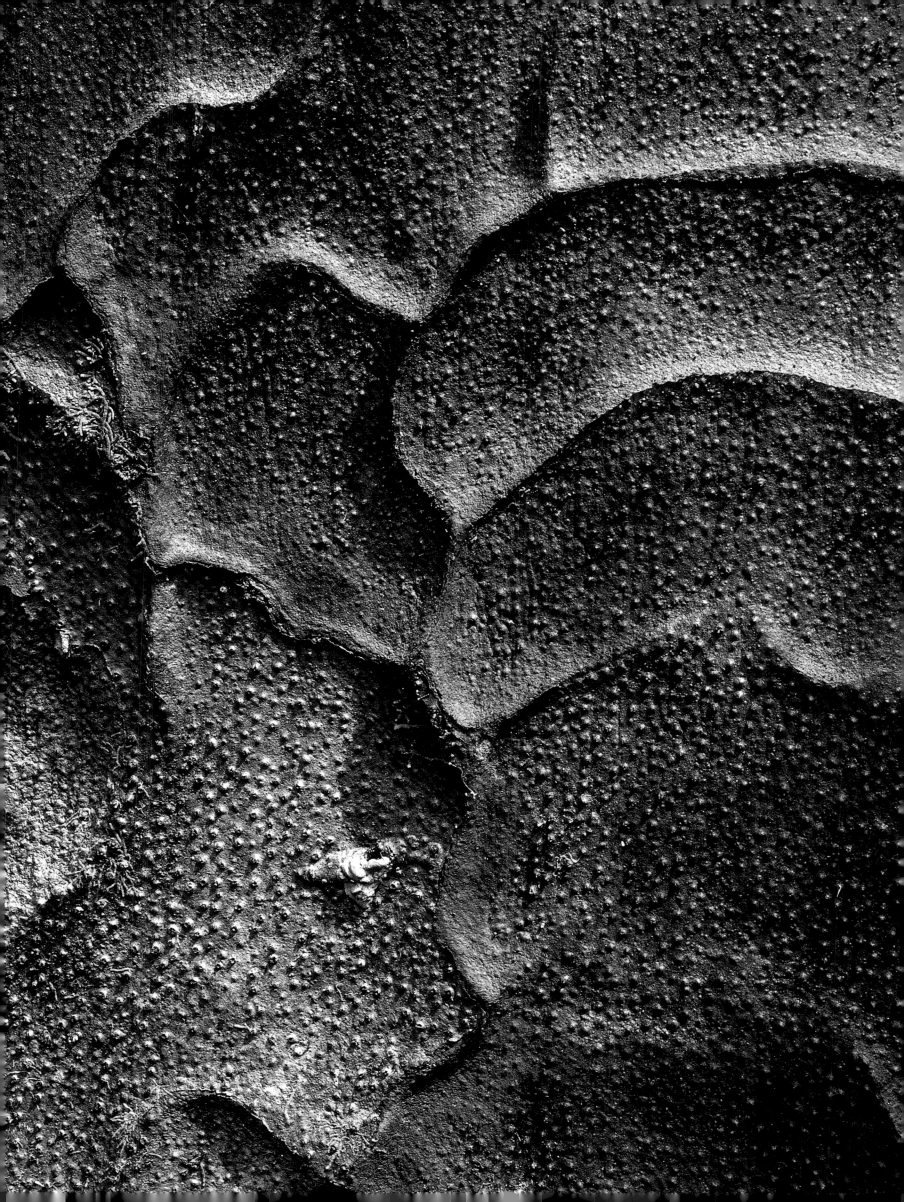

Araucarias

Araucarias, whose name derives from the region of Chile called Arauco, home to *Araucaria araucana*, or more familiarly the monkey puzzle tree, comprise forty or so primitive conifers, characteristic of the southern hemisphere: namely *Araucaria*, the *Aganthis* and the *Wollemia*. New Caledonia alone accounts for nearly half of all the species. The majority are trees with massive trunks that are used for their wood, their resin (for lacquers and varnishes) and sometimes for their edible nuts.

1. *Agathis robusta*
   PARC VIGIER, NICE (FRANCE)

2. *Agathis borneensis*
   KEBUN RAYA BOGOR (INDONESIA)

3. *Agathis lanceolata*
   MONT KOGHIS (NEW CALEDONIA)

4. *Agathis ovata*
   MONTS DZUMAC (NEW CALEDONIA)

5. *Wollemia nobilis*
   MONT ANNAN BOTANIC GARDEN (AUSTRALIA)

6. *Araucaria hunsteinii*
   KEW GARDENS, RICHMOND (UK)

7. *Araucaria heterophylla*
   NICE (FRANCE)

8. *Araucaria angustifolia*
   ANTIBES (FRANCE)

9. *Araucaria araucana*
   KEW GARDENS, RICHMOND (UK)

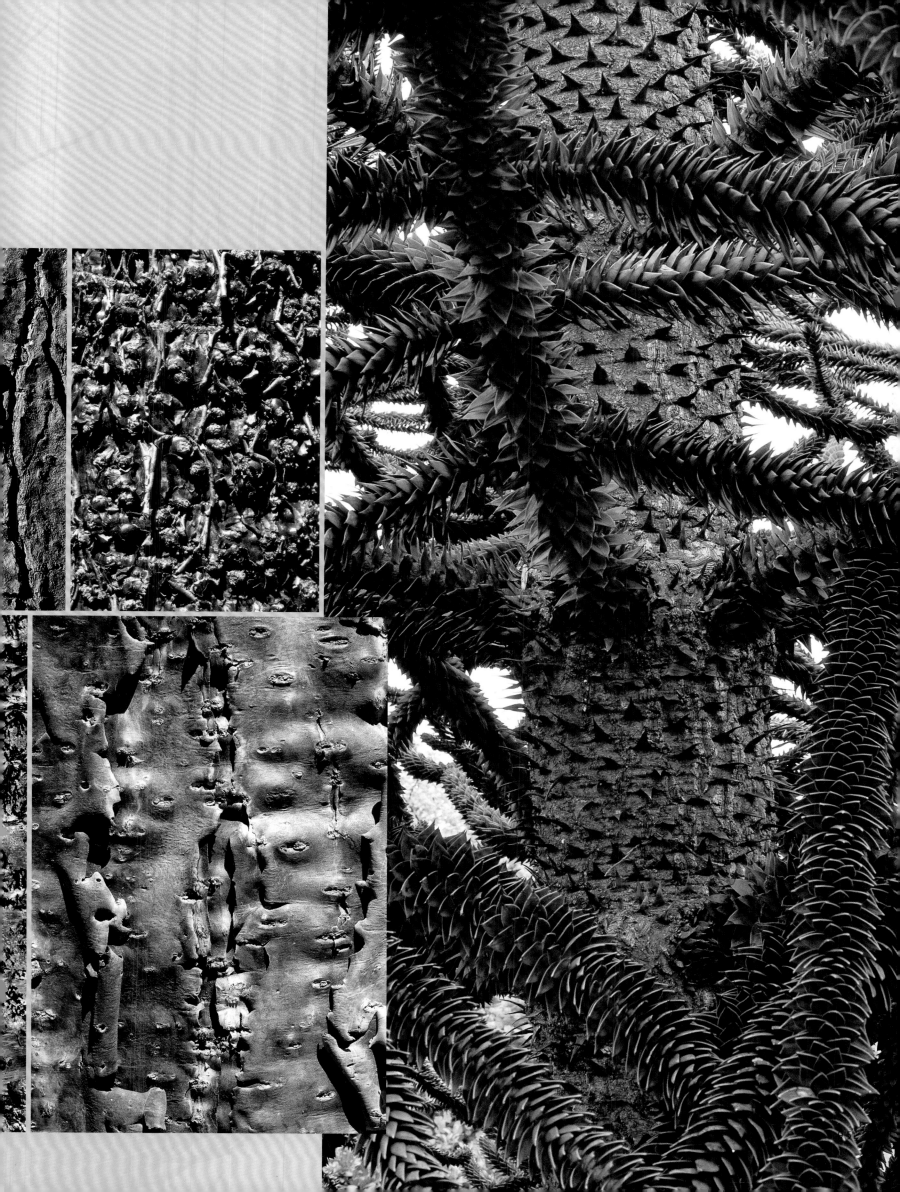

↗ *Xanthorrhoea australis* in its natural habitat after a bush fire. ROCKY CAPE NATIONAL PARK, TASMANIA (AUSTRALIA)

GRASS TREE

Xanthorrhoea australis

This curious giant perennial in the form of a tree is really a living fossil, whose growth is barely more than 1m (3ft) in 100 years. Of the 30 species native to Australia, this is the most southerly of all, found in the south-east and in Tasmania. It is a pyrophyte: fires stimulate the growth of leaves and flowers. It is also a plant that is very important to Aboriginal life. The leaf stems, the tips of the shoots and the roots are all edible. The flowers, rich in nectar, were gathered for sweetening and scenting water while the flower stalks were used for spears or to rub together, in the ancient method, to create fire. The genus name Xanthorrhoea means 'yellow liquid' in Greek, alluding to the resin it produces that is used variously for glue, to weatherproof, as a varnish or for incense. The Germans even used it for explosives in the First World War.

→
Xanthorrhoea australis
ROCKY CAPE NATIONAL PARK,
TASMANIA (AUSTRALIA)

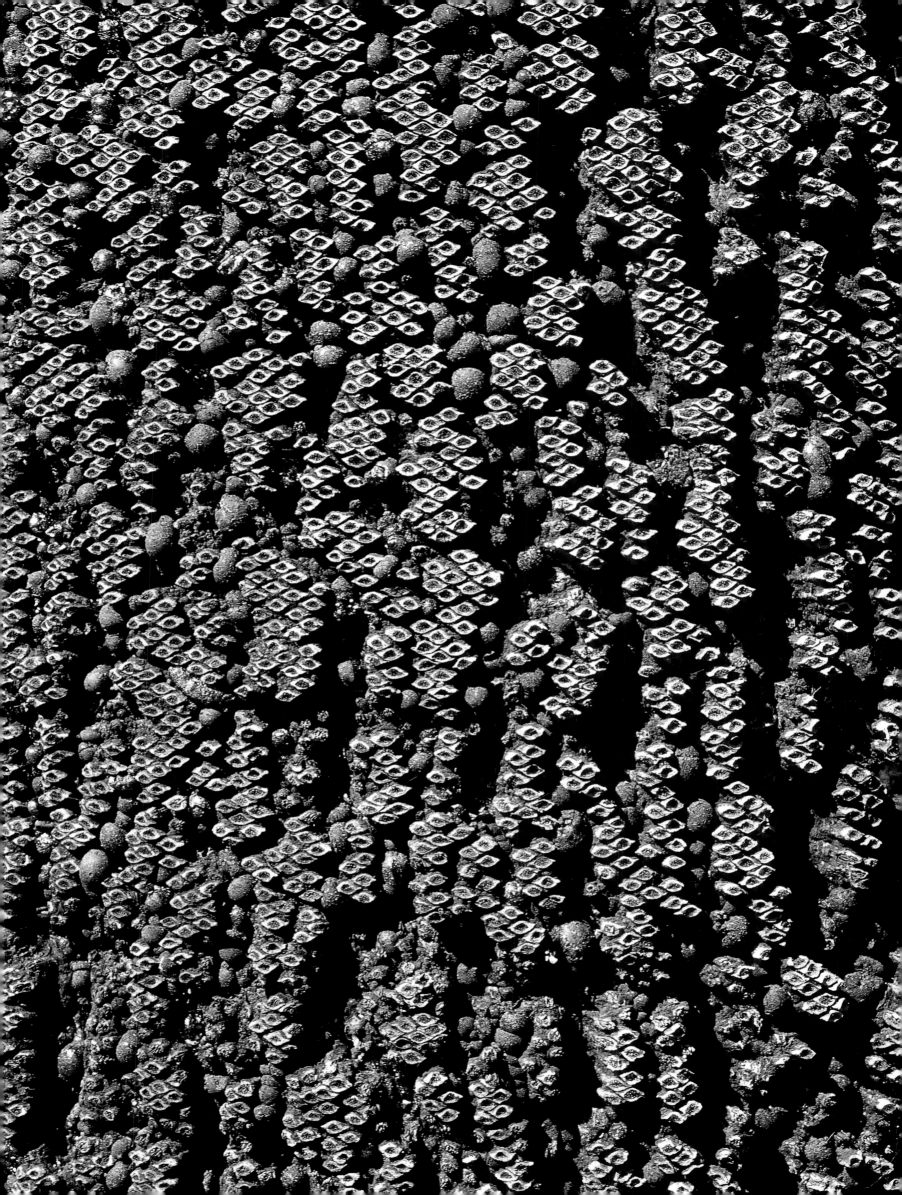

↗ The fleeting colours of the twisted trunks of *Eucalyptus coccifera*. LAKE FENTON, MTOUNT FIELD NATIONAL PARK, TASMANIA (AUSTRALIA)

(MYRTACEAE FAMILY)

TASMANIAN SNOW GUM

Eucalyptus coccifera

Perched in the alpine forests on the central plateau and southern mountains of Tasmania, at the extreme limit of the tree line (1,300m/430ft), this little tree is a fantastic example of how eucalyptus can cope with extreme temperatures: it survives 150 days of frost a year. In the best conditions, it can grow up to 30m (100ft) tall. In autumn, the brilliant leaf colours of Australia's only winter-deciduous tree *Nothofagus gunnii* clothe the mountains. As if spurred on by this festival of colours, the Tasmanian snow gum reveals the glories of its bark: sunshine colours to begin with, turning quickly to a more wintry grey brown. Its species name, *coccifera*, refers to the insect (*coccus*) that infested some of the first species of the tree to be collected in Tasmania.

↗ Young trunk of *Eucalyptus coccifera*. Lake Skinner, Tasmania (Australia)

↗ *Eucalyptus coccifera*
Cradle Mountain-Lake St Clair National Park, Tasmania (Australia)

↗ *Eucalyptus coccifera*
Lake Skinner, Tasmania (Australia)

SWAMP MALLEE

Eucalyptus spathulata

The species *spathulata* – referring to its spatula shaped leaves – is a small eucalyptus growing widely in south-west Australia. It has smooth, colourful bark and it tolerates frost, salt, drought and very damp conditions, the latter earning it the common name, swamp mallee. Its toughness means that it is relatively unthreatened by the major environmental catastrophe facing Australia: the increasing salinity of its soil. Trees, big consumers of water, maintain the water table that has been present in the subsoil of Australia, underneath a layer of salt, for thousands of years. After deforestation, the water tends to rise to the surface, bringing the salt with it, which then contaminates the rooting area of the soil. Intensive farming also encourages this process, which can threaten many hundreds of species with extinction.

↗ Bright colours of the very
young bark.

←
→ *Eucalyptus spathulata*
Wildflower Garden, Black Hill Conservation Park,
Adélaide, Southern Australia (Australia)

↗ *Eucalyptus camaldulensis*, the sinuous red gum whose branches extend more than 40m (130ft). Dunkeld, Victoria (Australia).

RIVER RED GUM

Eucalyptus camaldulensis

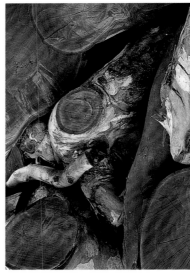

This eucalyptus, found throughout Australia, is particularly prevalent along the vast wetlands of the Murray Basin. Nevertheless, its name, *camaldulensis*, is in homage to the Italian Count of Camaldoli, whose gardens in Naples (*Hortus Camaldulensis di Napoli*) are home to many specimens and from which the first specimen came to be described. A very fast-growing tree, it has been widely planted throughout the world for its hard red wood. An essential tree for the Aborigines, its wood was ideal for heating and for making didgeridoos and its bark was used for making canoes, drinking containers and clothes, while its sap and leaves were employed for treating fevers, sore throats and diarrhoea. It is one of the small group of eucalyptus whose leaves are eaten by koala bears.

↗→ *Eucalyptus camaldulensis*
typical red wood.
Nice, (France)

SCRIBBLY GUM

Eucalyptus sclerophylla

Certain species of tree have long fascinated the Aborigines: their trunks reveal mysterious writing, a kind of zigzag scribbling, which no-one knows how to interpret. In the 1930s Tom Greaves succeeded in partially solving the enigma of this bush graffiti: a tiny butterfly had just laid its eggs between the old and new bark. The larvae (*Ogmograptis scribula*) create little tunnels in the new bark, which are revealed as the old bark falls away. These fascinating traces are a real key to identification for botanists. From it they have found at least five distinctive forms of scribbling, and more than 20 scribbly gum trees, of which this one grows mainly in the Blue Mountains to the west of Sydney. We had to wait till 2005 to capture and identify the lifecycle of the butterfly in question.

←
→ *Eucalyptus sclerophylla*
BLUE MOUNTAINS NATIONAL PARK,
NEW SOUTH WALES [AUSTRALIA]

DORRIGO WHITE GUM

Eucalyptus dorrigoensis

This majestic eucalyptus originates in the small region of Dorrigo in the north of New South Wales in Australia. The natural population is isolated and sparse, so this species is very vulnerable. The ghostly silhouette creates an unforgettable spectacle. Just before it loses its bark, the branches take on a rosy hue. Great cylindrical rolls of loose bark, attached at one end to the trunk of the tree, float in the breeze before they fall and cover the ground, crackling under foot. The young bark, yellow at the outset, turns progressively whiter and whiter, giving rise to its common name.

←↗ *Eucalyptus dorrigoensis*
JARDIN BOTANIQUE DE LA VILLA THURET
INRA ANTIBES (FRANCE)

← *Angophora costata* ROYAL BOTANIC GARDENS, SYDNEY, NEW SOUTH WALES (AUSTRALIA)

↓ The bark of *Angophora costata* before and after peeling. JARDIN BOTANIQUE DE LA VILLA THURET, INRA ANTIBES (FRANCE)

SYDNEY RED GUM

Angophora costata

There are just about a dozen species of *Angophora*, confined to the east side of Australia. At first glance, there are many that look like eucalyptus. However, even if they are named as such, they are different by virtue of their opposite leaves and an open flower, without the little cap that covers the stamens of a eucalyptus. *Angophora costata* means, in Greek, having 'ribbed goblets', alluding to the characteristic form of its fruit. When it loses its old grey bark, the trunk reveals a range of colours. From a fleeting blue-green, the bark turns rapidly yellow, then orange, then salmon pink.

Eucalyptus

The genus *Eucalyptus*, with its wide range of 700 species, almost all from Australia, is a worthy representative of the beautiful Myrtle family. Its name in Greek means 'well covered' referring to the little cap on all its button flowers. It is the tallest flowering tree (more than 100m/330ft in the case of *E. regnas*). Used in the timber industry, for paper, medicine and perfume, it is planted frequently in the tropical and temperate regions of the world.

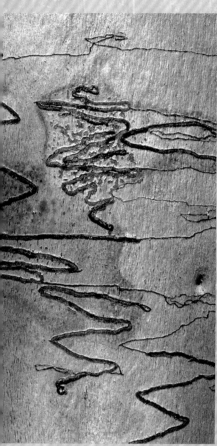

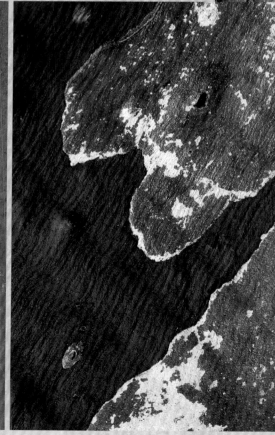

1. *Eucalyptus rossii*
   AUSTRALIAN NATIONAL
   BOTANIC GARDENS,
   CANBERRA (AUSTRALIA)

2. *Eucalyptus deglupta*
   FAIRCHILD, CORAL GABLES
   (USA)

3. *Eucalyptus torelliana*
   KEBUN RAYA CIBODAS
   (INDONESIA)

4. *Eucalyptus coccifera*
   LAKE SKINNER, TASMANIA
   (AUSTRALIA)

5. *Eucalyptus mannifera*
   AUSTRALIAN NATIONAL
   BOTANIC GARDENS,
   CANBERRA (AUSTRALIA)

6. *Eucalyptus rubiginosa*
   ROYAL BOTANIC GARDENS,
   SYDNEY (AUSTRALIA)

7. *Eucalyptus tesselaris*
   AUSTRALIAN NATIONAL
   BOTANIC GARDENS,
   CANBERRA (AUSTRALIA)

8. *Eucalyptus sideroxylon*
   JARDIN BOTANIQUE VILLA
   THURET, ANTIBES
   (FRANCE)

9. *Eucalyptus moluccana*
   ROYAL BOTANIC GARDENS,
   SYDNEY (AUSTRALIA)

10. *Eucalyptus delegatensis*
    WAKEHURST PLACE,
    ARDINGLY (UK)

11. *Eucalyptus globulus*
    NICE (FRANCE)

12. *Eucalyptus spathulata*
    WILDFLOWER GARDEN,
    ADÉLAIDE (AUSTRALIA)

SPOTTED GUM

Corymbia maculata

The spotted gum grows on the east coast of Australia. Its name, coming from the Latin, *maculosus*, or 'spotted', refers to the marks on the bark that resemble those of the plane tree. The old, orange-coloured bark peels off at the beginning of summer, leaving behind asymmetrical, rounded, green, then grey-white and finally yellow, shapes. Its very hard wood is used in many forms of timber construction. The nectar-rich flowers make excellent honey. Since the end of the 20th century, experts have transferred more than 100 eucalyptus, including this one, into the *Corymbia* genus. It differs in the structure of its flower, a corymb, in which the flowers, regardless of the length of their stems, are on the same plane.

←
→ The intense colours of *Corymbia maculata* a few days before the bark renews itself.
SERRE DE LA MADONE, MENTON (FRANCE)

The evolving bark throughout the year

↗ *Corymbia maculata* JARDIN BOTANIQUE DE LA VILLA THURET, INRA ANTIBES (FRANCE)

LEMON-SCENTED GUM

Corymbia citriodora

The lemon-scented gum, originating in the north-east of Australia, is a gift to both perfume makers and doctors. Its leaves, which release a strong scent of lemon, are used in herbal medicine to cure colds, sore throats and chest infections. It is also an effective natural anti-mosquito treatment. The result of the bark peeling at the beginning of the summer is, for this species alone, a magical moment. From pure white, the bark suddenly takes on rosy tints. It peels off from cracks that resemble a zip, revealing an unexpected blue colouring. From the first moments of being exposed to the sun, a symphony of colour changes strikes up and, in the space of a few weeks, the whole bark turns grey-white, then yellow, then a pale salmon colour.

↗→
Corymbia citriodora
JARDIN BOTANIQUE DE LA VILLA
THURET, INRA ANTIBES (FRANCE)

Different phases of colour change throughout the year

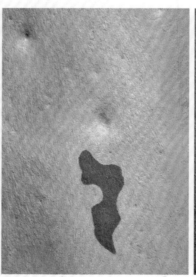

↗ *Corymbia citriodora* JARDIN BOTANIQUE DE LA VILLA THURET, INRA ANTIBES (FRANCE)

BROAD-LEAVED PAPERBARK TREE

Melaleuca quinquenervia

Among the 250 species of Melaleuca, the broad-leaved paperbark tree is undoubtedly one of the best known. The name comes from the Greek *melas* (black) and *leukos* (white), alluding to the black trunk and white branches of some trees after a forest fire. The species name refers to the characteristic leaves with their five almost parallel veins. It likes the humid parts of the east coats of Australia, New Guinea and New Caledonia. It holds an important place in the daily life of the natives. The thick papery bark serves to insulate the traditional huts, to cook *en papillote* and to sweeten Kanak delicacies. The leaves, rich in essential oils, are used to treat lung infections. Unfortunately, the broad-leaved paperbark is very invasive and can destroy fragile eco-systems like those of the Everglades in the south of Florida.

↑ →
Melaleuca quinquenervia is still distilled at Bouluparis in New Caledonia to obtain its precious essential oils.
GRANDE TERRE (NEW CALEDONIA)

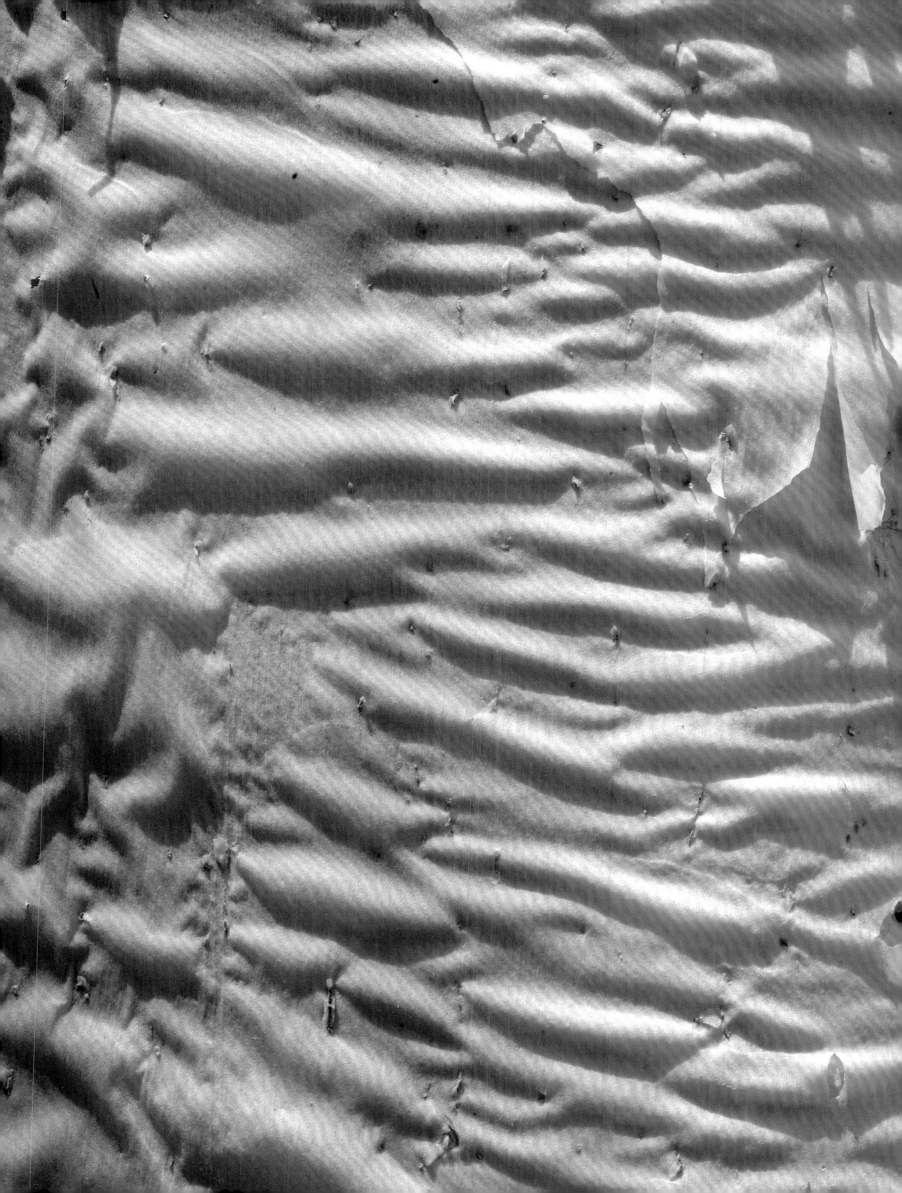

NARROW-LEAF BOTTLETREE

Brachychiton rupestris

The genus name comes from *brachy* (short) and *chiton* (coat), referring to the stinging filaments that surround the seeds. Once these filaments are removed, the seeds are edible. The bottletree is a rock plant, as its Latin name *rupestris*, or 'rocky', implies, which loves the stony soils of the dry regions of Queensland in Australia. During the rainy season, the plant's tissues swell with water. All you need do then is to pierce the bark to draw off a kind of nutritious jelly, much appreciated by the Aborigines. The trunk swells into a bottle shape with a diameter of more than 2m (6ft) in some cases. It is covered with characteristic photosynthetic bark which thickens and cracks as it ages, losing its green colour and hence its ability to photosynthesize. The Aborigines use the inner layer of bark, which is very fibrous, for making nets.

←
→ *Brachychiton rupestris*
ROYAL BOTANIC GARDENS, SYDNEY,
NEW SOUTH WALES (AUSTRALIA)

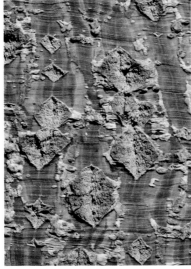

↗ *Brachychiton discolor*
JARDIN BOTANIQUE DE LA VILLA
THURET, INRA ANTIBES (FRANCE)

↗ *Brachychiton rupestris*
As it ages, the bark cracks and loses its chlorophyll.
ROYAL BOTANIC GARDENS, SYDNEY, NEW SOUTH WALES (AUSTRALIA)

HOOP PINE

Araucaria cunninghamii

In the 1820s, Alan Cunningham, the English explorer and botanist, discovered this pine in the tropical forests on the east coast of Australia. Its bark peels horizontally at regular intervals, rather like that of some ornamental cherry trees. Its common name, hoop pine, refers to the fine bark, unusual for a pine, which peels into circular shapes. Its high-quality wood has been widely used in the Australian plywood industry. Sadly, it grows very slowly (around 2cm / ¾ inch a year as an adult tree) and can take 200 years to produce cones, with the result that most of the natural plantations have been decimated. The resin, after it had been heated, was used by Aborigines as a fixative.

←
↗ *Araucaria cunninghamii*
KEBUN RAYA CIBODAS, WEST JAVA (INDONESIA)

ASIA

Phyllostachys pubescens,
Bamboo with a
thousand and one
uses, Bambouseraie
de Prafrance,
Générargues (France)

RAINBOW EUCALYPTUS

Eucalyptus deglupta

This splendid Mindanaon gum (or rainbow eucalyptus), from the island of the same name in the south-west of the Philippines, is the only eucalyptus originating in the northern hemisphere. It does equally well, however, in the forests of Indonesia and New Guinea. Its trunk, with its surreal colours, looks like something out of an artist's studio. Throughout its growing period, largely in the rainy season, the old bark peels off in several places to form fine sheets. It reveals, successively, pale green, dark green, blue-green, purplish and orange-red hues, resembling a rainbow (hence its common name). It is often planted to make *papier mache* and is also used in the construction industry. In the Philippines, the bark is used as a traditional remedy to combat fatigue.

↗→ *Eucalyptus deglupta*
multicoloured bark.
KEBUN RAYA BOGOR, WEST JAVA (INDONESIA)

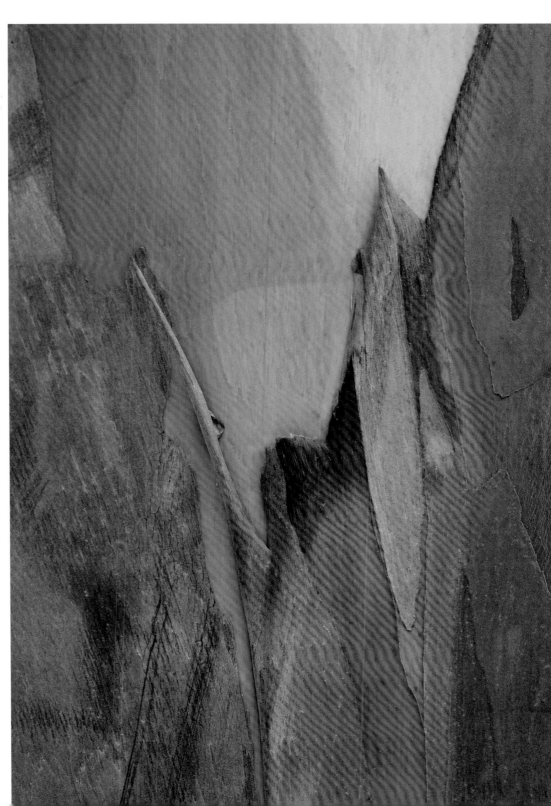

← *Eucalyptus deglupta*, a magnificent specimen with a ribbed trunk.
COL DE PUNCAK, WEST JAVA (INDONESIA)

SAGO PALM
Metroxylon sagu

The sago palm comes from South-East Asia (Indonesia, Malaysia, Philippines) and from Papua New Guinea. In Greek, *metroxylon* means 'heartwood', referring to the pith that is used for the pudding we know as sago. This palm tree is called monocarpic: it flowers and produces fruits only once in its life. At 10 to 15 years old, the sago palm is cut down, at the time when its reserves are at their greatest and just before it develops its massive flower. The trunk is opened up to remove the pith, which is beaten, washed and pressed to harvest the starchy grains that are found in the fibres. Doing well in marshy ground where no other species will grow, it is still the primary source of food for many indigenous peoples.

↗ *Metroxylon sagu*, the typically spiny bases of the palm fronds. KEBUN RAYA BOGOR, WEST JAVA (INDONESIA)

←
→ *Metroxylon sagu*
KEBUN RAYA BOGOR, WEST JAVA (INDONESIA)

LIPSTICK PALM

Cyrtostachys renda

This typical tropical palm is found widely in South-East Asia on the Malaysian peninsula and in Indonesia on Sumatra and Borneo. The sheath, leaf stalk and the midribs of these palms are bright orange-red, hence the common name, lipstick palm. It grows in clumps and forms big stands, in which the trunks photosynthesize. They resemble the canes of giant bamboos. Despite its great ornamental qualities, it has not been widely cultivated. With its need for heat (it does not tolerate temperatures lower than 100C/ 500F), it is difficult to grow successfully. The Chinese practice of *feng shui* recommends that it is planted at the entrance to a house. According to this ancient art, it will attract positive energy and help to bring wellbeing and good fortune to the householders.

→
← *Cyrtostachys renda*
KEBUN RAYA BOGOR, WEST JAVA (INDONESIA)

WEEPING FIG

Ficus benjamina

The genus *Ficus*, with more than 750 species, is characterized by its sap, a milky latex that can be toxic, which is used occasionally in the manufacture of rubber (*F. elastica*). Weeping figs come in various forms: climbers, shrubs or huge trees. The famous Great Banyan Tree in Calcutta covers more than 1.5 hectares (3.7 acres) and forms a forest of more than 2,500 trunks, all emanating from the same mother plant. The weeping fig, which is easy to cultivate and to look after, has rapidly become the most widely grown indoor plant in the world. However, in its native habitat (principally India and South-West Asia), it is a big tree able to reach heights of nearly 30m (100ft). It is often covered with a dense tracery of aerial roots, resembling the structure of the strangler fig. Beware, though, of the milky sap from its leaves, which has often been the cause of accidental poisoning.

↗ *Ficus tettensis*
SOUTPANSBERG, LIMPOPO
(SOUTH AFRICA)

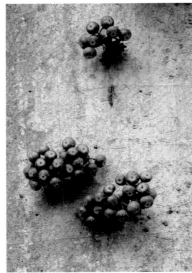

↗ *Ficus* cauliflory
KEBUN RAYA BOGOR, WEST JAVA
(INDONESIA)

→
← *Ficus benjamina*
with its dense covering
of aerial roots.
MIAMI, FLORIDA (USA)

CEYLON CINNAMON

Cinnamomum verum

From China to the Mediterranean, from Egyptian papyruses to the Bible, the spicy aroma of the bark of the cinnamon tree has formed part of our civilization for thousands of years, whether used for perfume, as a spice or as a remedy. Cinnamon flavours tea, warm wine, pastries, rice, meat, curries, vegetables and more. It is harvested in the rainy season, when the inner bark is at its most aromatic and also detaches itself most easily from the outer bark. Once dried, it forms the little cylinders resembling tiny canes we are familiar with. *Cinnamomum verum*, with its fine bark, and subtle, sweet perfume, is grown primarily in Sri Lanka in the form of a small clump-forming shrub. Chinese cinnamon (*C. aromaticum*) is thicker and more strongly perfumed; it is one of the famous Chinese blend of 'five spices'.

↗ *Cinnamomum verum*
in the middle of a tea plantation.
COL DE PUNCAK, WEST JAVA (INDONESIA)

↗ *Cinnamomum verum,*
the young leaves and the dried
cylinders of spicy bark.
COL DE PUNCAK, WEST JAVA (INDONESIA)

JAPANESE BANANA PLANT

Musa basjoo

The Latin name of the banana plant is a dedication to Antonio Musa, the celebrated doctor to the Popes and the crowned heads of 16th century Europe. There are around 50 species originating in Asia and the Pacific basin, cultivated throughout the world for their fruits. The Japanese banana plant owes its popularity more to its ornamental value than to its fruit, which is inedible. Originating in the Chinese subtropical regions of Yunnan and Szechuan, it is the hardiest of all the banana plants. The vigorous rhizome gives rise to shoots that rapidly create a dense population of new plants. Its pseudo-trunk, which is green and spongy, is often covered with yellow scars, the remains of old leaves, desiccated by the cold. Its fibre, used for centuries in Japan (where it was described for the first time), is employed in the textile industry and for making cords and ropes.

↗ *Musa basjoo*
GAMBOUSERAIE DE PRAFRANCE,
GÉNÉRARGUES (FRANCE)

↓ *Musa basjoo,* the fibrous and spongy bark. ST-JEAN-CAP-FERRAT (FRANCE)

↗ A flower of *Musa ornata* and a rack of bananas of *Musa acuminata.*
FAIRCHILD TROPICAL BOTANIC GARDEN,
CORAL GABLES, FLORIDA (USA)

MOSO BAMBOO

Phyllostachys pubescens

This giant perennial, nicknamed 'the people's friend' in China, is part of the daily life of millions of Asian people, who attribute almost 1,500 uses to it. With its combination of flexibility and strength, the bamboo has served as the ideal traditional construction material for houses, boats, scaffolding and so on. Moso is the most popular of all the Chinese bamboos. Rich in vitamins and fibres, its young shoots have played a key role in Asian cuisine for thousands of years. Very hardy, it can reach heights of over 20m (65 ft), at an astonishing growth rate of 5cm (2in) per hour! Its appearance is characterized by a sheath that rolls back to expose a cane covered in white powder.

How the canes develop

↗ *Phyllostachys pubescens* Bambouseraie de Prafrance, Générargues (France)

→
← *Phyllostachys pubescens,* the canes in full growth.
Bambouseraie de Prafrance, Générargues (France)

Bamboos

The bamboo is a giant perennial used throughout thousands of years in Asia, where its diversity is greatest, and also in other continents apart from Europe. There are more than 1,500 species, the majority of which are tropical, but almost one fifth are considered hardy. Some species are distinguished by the impressive height of the canes, their rapid rate of growth (more than 1m/3ft a day) or their unusual, irregular flowering.

1. *Gigantochloa atroviolacea*
   KEBUN RAYA BOGOR (INDONESIA)

2. *Dendrocalamus asper*
   ST-JEAN-CAP-FERRAT (FRANCE)

3. *Phyllostachys pubescens* 'Bicolor'
   LA BAMBOUSERAIE, GÉNÉRARGUES (FRANCE)

4. *Dendrocalamus giganteus*
   KEBUN RAYA BOGOR (INDONESIA)

5. *Phyllostachys pubescens* 'Heterocycla'
   LA BAMBOUSERAIE, GÉNÉRARGUES (FRANCE)

6. *Phyllostachys bambusoides* 'Castillonis Inversa'
   LA BAMBOUSERAIE, GÉNÉRARGUES (FRANCE)

7. *Bambusa vulgaris* 'Vitatta'
   JARDIN BOTANIQUE DE LYON (FRANCE)

8. *Phyllostachys viridis* cv. 'Sulfurea'
   LA BAMBOUSERAIE, GÉNÉRARGUES (FRANCE)

9. *Phyllostachys viridis* cv. 'Sulfurea'
   LA BAMBOUSERAIE, GÉNÉRARGUES (FRANCE)

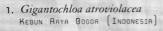

1	2	3	4	5	9
	6	7	8		

TIBETAN CHERRY

Prunus serrula

There are more than 200 species of Prunus, principally from the temperate regions of the northern hemisphere. They are cultivated for their fruits (plum, cherry, apricot, peach), their nuts (almond) or simply for their wonderful displays of flowers, like the many flowering Japanese cherries. The Tibetan cherry is distinguished by its reddish bark, which brings a welcome touch of colour to gardens in winter. Its late-flowering, small white blossoms tend to be hidden by the leaves. It was discovered in the mountains of the south-west of China by Ernest Wilson and then introduced to Europe at the beginning of the 20th century. Its species name, *serrula*, means 'little saw' in Latin, referring to the toothed edges to its leaves, which turn gold-red in autumn.

↗ *Prunus maackii*
WESTONBIRT ARBORETUM, TETBURY (UK)

↗ *Prunus rufa*
HERGEST CROFT GARDENS, KINGTON (UK)

→
← *Prunus serrula*
JARDIN DU BOIS MARQUIS, VERNIOZ (FRANCE)

CHINESE RED BIRCH

Betula albosinensis

This astonishing birch is a native of the deciduous forests in the centre of China. Introduced to the West by the celebrated plant hunter Ernest Wilson, it is one of the tallest birches, reaching more than 30m (100ft) in height in its natural habitat. Unlike the majority of birches, which are characterized by their silver, grey or pale bark, the Chinese red birch displays a whole range of surprising colours. Its bark can take on brownish-red, orange, chocolate and even rose and purplish tints. Its bright gold autumn foliage is also very attractive.

→
← *Betula albosinensis*
with multicoloured, light-sensitive bark.
HERGEST CROFT GARDENS, KINGTON (UK)

HIMALAYAN BIRCH

Betula utilis

The classification of the birch genus is a real headache for botanists. Whether growing in the wild or planted, they hybridize very readily, which makes for many forms and a great deal of confusion. The Himalayan birches are represented by the species *B. utilis*, which grows in Nepal at high altitudes (more than 4,000m/13,000ft). Its Latin name *utilis*, or 'useful', refers to its multiple uses including roofing and paper. The Himalayan birch was discovered at the beginning of the 19th century by the botanist Nathaniel Wallich, then director of the Botanic Gardens of Calcutta. Its bark creates a great range of colours along the Himalayan mountain chain: pure white (*var. jacquemontii*), dark greyish-purple (*var. prattii*) and pastel, cream, rose or orange-red (species *utilis and var. utilis*).

← *Betula utilis* var. *jacquemontii*, luminous pure white bark.
SIR HAROLD HILLIER GARDENS, AMPFIELD (UK)

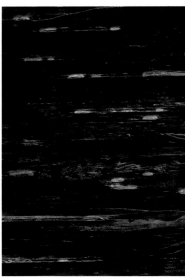

↗ *Betula utilis*
SIR HAROLD HILLIER GARDENS, AMPFIELD (UK)

↗ *Betula utilis* var. *utilis*
HERGEST CROFT GARDENS, KINGTON (UK)

↗ *Betula utilis* var. *prattii*
HERGEST CROFT GARDENS, KINGTON (UK)

→
Betula utilis var. *jacquemontii*
JARDIN DU BOIS MARQUIS, VERNIOZ (FRANCE)

Birches

There are dozens of species of birch, all originating in the cold and temperate regions of the northern hemisphere. These are very hardy trees, able to grow in poor soils and in the freezing cold of the Arctic. Like the hazel, alder and hornbeam, the birch belongs to the *Betulaceae* family, of which it is the main genus. Venerated by many different peoples of the world, it serves as shelter, a source of heat and lighting, a medicine and a refreshing drink.

1. *Betula delavayi*
WESTONBIRT ARBORETUM,
TETBURY (UK)

2. *Betula* 'Hergest'
HERGEST CROFT GARDENS
KINGTON (UK)

3. *Betula utilis*
WAKEHURST PLACE,
ARDINGLY (UK)

4. *Betula utilis* var. *prattii*
WESTONBIRT ARBORETUM,
TETBURY (UK)

5. *Betula forrestii*
HILLIER GARDENS
AMPFIELD (UK)

6. *Betula costata*
WESTONBIRT ARBORETUM,
TETBURY (UK)

7. *Betula albosinensis*
HERGEST CROFT GARDENS,
KINGTON (UK)

8. *Betula grossa*
WAKEHURST PLACE,
ARDINGLY (UK)

9. *Betula papyrifera*
HERGEST CROFT GARDENS,
KINGTON (UK)

10. *Betula* ' Dick Banks'
HERGEST CROFT GARDENS
KINGTON (UK)

11. *Betula davurica*
ARNOLD ARBORETUM BOSTON
(USA)

12. *Betula* sp.
WAKEHURST PLACE
ARDINGLY (UK)

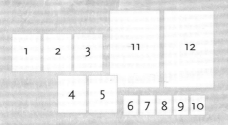

CHINESE ZELKOVA

Zelkova sinica

In the Pliocene epoch, between two and five million years ago, the zelkova formed great forests all over the northern hemisphere until the Ice Age reduced its terrain. There now remains only a half dozen species in isolated groups in the islands of the Mediterranean (Sicily, Crete), in the Caucasus and in the eastern part of Asia. Its common name comes from the word *tselkwa* given to the local species, *Z. carpinifolia* (Siberian elm), by Caucasians. The species, *sinica*, originating in China, was discovered by Ernest Wilson at the beginning of the 20th century. Just like the elm, to which it is closely related, it is one of the best species for creating bonsai forms. Its young spring foliage is rose-tinted, flaring red later in the autumn.

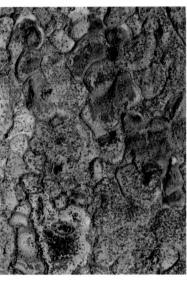

↗ *Zelkova serrata*
ARNOLD ARBORETUM OF HARVARD UNIVERSITY, BOSTON, MASSACHUSETTS (USA)

↗ *Ulmus parvifolia*, a close cousin.
ADELAIDE, SOUTHERN AUSTRALIA (AUSTRALIA)

→
← *Zelkova sinica*
ARNOLD ARBORETUM OF HARVARD UNIVERSITY, BOSTON, MASSACHUSETTS (USA)

LACEBARK PINE

Pinus bungeana

This remarkable pine with its divided trunk was found in the temple gardens in Beijing in 1831 by the Russian botanist, Alexander von Bunge, whose name is given to more than a hundred oriental plants. Native to the central and northern parts of China, it is often planted in Buddhist temples or in cemeteries. It grows very slowly – one reason why it has not been more widely planted. You need to be patient to admire its camouflage-like bark, which closely resembles that of the plane tree. When the bark peels into its characteristic rounded shapes, it reveals its green and brown trunk, spotted with yellow and reddish-brown. As it ages, the bark tends to whiten.

↗ As the seasons and weather change, the bark changes colour.

→
← *Pinus bungeana*
JARDIN BOTANIQUE
DE LA VILLE DE LYON (FRANCE)

JAPANESE STEWARTIA

Stewartia pseudocamellia

A close relative of the tea plant (*Camellia sinensis*), the Japanese Stewartia is a tree of about 15m (50ft) in height, found in the central forests of Japan, from the south of Honshu to Kyushu and Shukoku, but also in Korea, where it shows a better resistance to the cold. It is attractive right through the year. In summer it is covered in fleeting white flowers, similar to those of the camellia (its name in Japanese, *natsutsubaki*, means 'summer-flowering camellia'). In autumn, once the leaves have fallen, the trunk displays astonishing orange-red marks. The Latin name pays tribute to John Stuart, the 3rd Earl of Bute, a well-known botanist and former Prime Minister under George III, who helped found the Royal Botanic Gardens at Kew.

↗ *Stewartia monadelpha*
WESTONBIRT ARBORETUM,
TETBURY (UK)

↗ *Stewartia sinensis*
ROYAL BOTANIC GARDENS KEW,
WAKEHURST PLACE, ARDINGLY (UK)

←
→ *Stewartia pseudocamelia*
ARNOLD ARBORETUM OF HARVARD UNIVERSITY,
BOSTON, MASSACHUSETTS (USA)

NATCHEZ CRAPE MYRTLE

Lagerstroemia 'Natchez' (*L. indica* 'Pink Lace' x *L. fauriei*)

The genus *Lagerstroemia* contains 50 or so species of very ornamental trees and shrubs, principally from South-East Asia. The name pays homage to Magnus von Lagerstrom, director of the Swedish East India Company. He collected a great many Asiatic plants for his friend, Linnaeus, the Swedish naturalist and the founder of plant nomenclature as we know it. The crape myrtle (*L. indica*), though originating in China, has been widely planted in India for its excellent quality of wood and its delightful flowers resembling those of lilac. In the 1950s the hardier *L. fauriei* was found on the island of Yakushima in the south of Japan. The Americans decided to cross these two plants, giving rise to the cultivar, 'Natchez', much admired for its very ornamental red bark.

↑ *Lagerstroemia* 'Natchez' Brooklyn Botanic Garden, New York (USA)

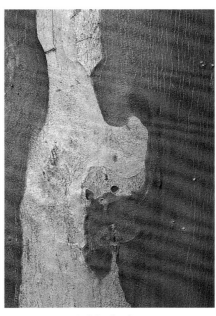

↗ *Lagerstroemia speciosa*
Kebun Raya Bogor,
West Java (Indonesia)

↗ *Lagerstroemia* 'Natchez'
Brooklyn Botanic Garden,
New York (USA)

↗ *Lagerstroemia duperreana*
Kebun Raya Bogor,
West Java (Indonesia)

PAPERBARK MAPLE

Acer griseum

This little maple with its cinnamon bark was discovered by the famous English botanist, Ernest Wilson, in Szechuan, in the central part of China. In 1901 he introduced this remarkable species into England for the nursery Veitch, always on the look out for new plants. Despite its very slow growth rate, it is often used as an ornamental tree, largely for its brownish-red bark, which peels in large fragments that roll up like a cinnamon stick. It gets its Latin name from the downy and greyish aspect of its winged fruits and of its leaves. These are composed of three leaflets and turn a clear red in autumn.

←
→ *Acer griseum*
ARNOLD ARBORETUM OF HARVARD UNIVERSITY,
BOSTON, MASSACHUSETTS (USA)

PERE DAVID'S MAPLE

Acer davidii

Originating in high-altitude forests in the centre and west of China, this tree is the most widely grown of the snakebark maples. It was discovered in 1879 by Father Armand David, an enthusiastic botanist, who sent samples from China to the *Jardins des Plantes* in Paris. Its green-and-white striped bark is striking in winter. Its foliage is also striking: reddish bronze in spring, dark green in summer and then yellow in autumn. Its wide natural range and its predisposition for hybridizing explains the huge diversity of forms in this species. In some cultivars like A. d. 'Rosalie' the colour of the bark changes with the seasons: green in summer, red and white striped in winter.

← *Acer davidii*
in its autumn guise.
ARBORETUM NATIONAL DES BARRES,
NOGENT-SUR-VERNISSON (FRANCE)

→
Acer davidii
JARDIN DU BOIS MARQUIS,
VERNIOZ (FRANCE)

Maples

There are about 120 species of maple all originating in the temperate climates of the northern hemisphere, the great majority (three-quarters of the species) from Asia or North America. They are known for their hand-shaped leaves, which colour the autumn landscape throughout the world. Their curious winged fruits turn like the blades of a helicopter. Twenty or so of the maples known as snakebark reveal striking bark striped with vertical coloured lines.

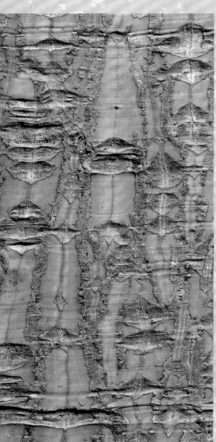

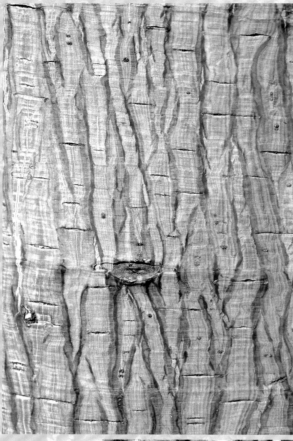

1. *Acer rufinerve*
'Albolimbatum'
HILLIER GARDENS,
AMPFIELD (UK)

2. *Acer* x *conspicuum*
'Silver Cardinal'
JARDIN DU BOIS MARQUIS,
VERNIOZ (FRANCE)

3. *Acer capillipes*
HILLIER GARDENS,
AMPFIELD (UK)

4. *Acer* x *conspicuum*
'Phoenix'
JARDIN DU BOIS MARQUIS,
VERNIOZ (FRANCE)

5. *Acer davidii*
JARDIN DU BOIS MARQUIS,
VERNIOZ (FRANCE)

6. *Acer griseum*
WAKEHURST PLACE,
ARDINGLY (UK)

7. *Acer morifolium*
WESTONBIRT ARBORETUM,
TETBURY (UK)

8. *Acer miyabei*
WESTONBIRT ARBORETUM,
TETBURY (UK)

9. *Acer pensylvanicum*
'Erythrocladum'
HILLIER GARDENS,
AMPFIELD (UK)

10. *Acer triflorum*
ARNOLD ARBORETUM, BOSTON
(USA)

11. *Acer griseum*
KEW GARDENS,
RICHMOND (UK)

12. *Acer rubescens*
HILLIER GARDENS,
AMPFIELD (UK)

| 1 | 2 | 3 | | 11 | 12 |

| | 4 | 5 | | 6 7 8 9 10 | |

PERSIAN IRONWOOD

Parrotia persica

The only species in the *Parrotia* genus, Persian ironwood originates in the north of Iran and the Caucasus. It is a very decorative tree, often with a branching trunk, offering a broad colour palette according to the season. In winter, it is covered with red, petal-less flowers and reveals a bark covered with green, yellow, orange and grey marks. In spring, the new foliage is purple, turning pale green later. The final triumph is in autumn: the leaves turn yellow, orange, red and bronze, while keeping some subtle trace of green. The name pays tribute to the German doctor, F.W. von Parrot, who in 1811, aged 20, explored and mapped the Caucasus. In 1821, his was the first recorded ascent of Mount Ararat, where Noah's Ark is said to have rested during the Great Flood.

↗ *Parrotia persica*
BROOKLYN BOTANIC GARDEN,
NEW YORK (USA)

↗ *Parrotia persica*
BROOKLYN BOTANIC GARDEN, NEW YORK (USA)

↗ *Parrotia persica*
ROYAL BOTANICAL GARDENS KEW, RICHMOND (UK)

Gleditsia caspica
ARNOLD ARBORETUM OF HARVARD UNIVERSITY,
BOSTON, MASSACHUSETTS (USA)

← *Gleditsia triacanthos*, American cousin of the
Caspian locust tree. ARNOLD ARBORETUM OF HARVARD
UNIVERSITY, BOSTON, MASSACHUSETTS (USA)

CASPIAN LOCUST TREE

Gleditsia caspica

The long, fine, groups of spines are typical of the genus *Gleditsia*. There are a dozen deciduous species in the genus, some in America but most of them in Asia. The Caspian locust tree, native to the north of Iran and the Trans-Caucasian region, is rarely more than 10–12m (33–40ft) in height. It trunk and branches are covered, when young, with white or reddish spines. It owes its Latin name to the German botanist, John Gottlieb Gleditsch, the former director of the Berlin Botanic Gardens and the author of numerous botanical and horticultural works in the 18th century.

AFRICA

Adansonia digitata,
with its huge trunk
measuring nearly 33m
(100ft) wide, the
Sagole baobab is one
of the biggest trees
in the world.
LIMPOPO (SOUTH AFRICA)

SOCOTRA DRAGON TREE

Dracaena cinnabari

The common name of this dragon tree comes from the Greek *draikaina* (female dragon) and *cinnabari* (cinnabar – red mercury), alluding to its blood red resin. Symbolic of the island of Socotra (Yemen), it has an important role in the daily life of the islanders. The drops of resin are harvested for medical purposes: to stop haemorrhages, treat conjunctivitis and help wounds to heal. The leaves, flowers and fruit are a valuable source of fodder for animals. The leaf fibres are also used to make very strong rope while the nectar-rich flowers produce the best honey in the world. Sadly, the increasing dryness of the island's climate and the over-population of goats, along with the recent over-exploitation of the resin and use of the wood for beehives, has threatened its survival.

↗ *Dracaena cinnabari,* the traditional harvesting of the dragon tree's red resin. SOCOTRA (YEMEN)

←
→ *Dracaena cinnabari*
a forest of old dragon trees in Hamadero. SOCOTRA (YEMEN)

FRANKINCENSE TREE

Boswellia elongata

Socotra is a Yemenite island to the east of the Horn of Africa. In this little botanical paradise you can find eight of the 24 species of incense trees growing in the world. The Yemen has always been the major source of incense, a precious commodity that has always been valued higher even than gold. The drops of resin are usually harvested after making a nick in the inner bark where the veins of resin are found. *Boswellia elongata* does not provide commercial quality incense. However, the Socotran islanders chew it as a mouth disinfectant and burn it, along with the outer bark, both to perfume and purify the air and to drive way evil spirits. In pottery, the resin is also used as glue or mastic while the smoke of the dead wood produces a mahogany colour. In times of famine, the leaves are used as fodder for animals.

↗ *Boswellia ameero*
SOCOTRA (YEMEN)

↗ *Boswellia socotrana,* pearls of incense at the foot of the tree and in the Yemen souks. (YEMEN)

↑
Boswellia elongata →
pure drops of incense before it crystallizes. SOCOTRA (YEMEN)

SOCOTRA STAR CHESTNUT

Sterculia africana var. *socotrana*

From its 15m (50ft) height, the African star chestnut, a native variety of Socotra (Yemen), dominates the remarkable flora of the island. Its characteristic fruit, star-shaped with three to five lobes, and its nourishing seeds, grilled or ground into flour, give rise to the common name of star chestnut. The entire tree provides the principal fodder for the islanders' animals. Its violet trunk takes on golden tints after the bark peels.

↗ *Sterculia africana* var. *socotrana*
the biggest tree on the island.
SOCOTRA (YEMEN)

↗ *Sterculia africana* var. *socotrana*
SOCOTRA (YEMEN)

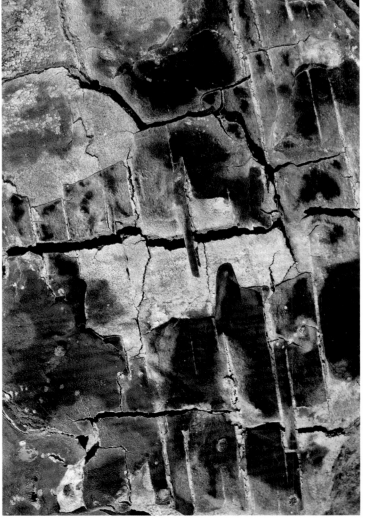

↗ *Sterculia rogersii*
LIMPOPO (SOUTH AFRICA)

SOCOTRA DESERT ROSE

Adenium socotranum

Adenium is a typical succulent, known as caudiciform – a plant that develops a bulbous base – growing in the tropical regions of Arabia and Africa. The name refers to the ancient town of Aden, the famous Yemenite port on the gulf of the same name. In March, the rose-tinted flowers colour the arid landscape of the island of Socotra, where it originates. Some species reach an impressive height (5m/16ft tall by 2m/6ft wide). Its medicinal juice disinfects wounds, soothes scorpion bites, protects animals against ticks or serves as bait for fishing.

←↗ *Adenium socotranum*
with a lagoon beyond. SOCOTRA (YEMEN)

ABYSSINIAN BANANA

Ensete ventricosum

Unlike the genus *Musa* (the true banana plant), with which this one has been grouped for several decades, the Abyssinian banana takes four to five years to mature, flower and then die, without putting out any new shoots. It can be distinguished by its swollen trunk and the rose-coloured main rib of its leaf. This giant perennial grows from the tropical regions of South Africa and up to Ethiopia. It has an important role in the life of the Gurages, the ethnic people of Ethiopia known more commonly as the Ensete people. They use the leaves of the Abyssinian banana for funeral ceremonies and for medicine. The root, rich in starch, is used to make bread known as 'kocho' and provides their principal source of carbohydrate. The trunk, edible when young and full of fibre, is also used to make rope and various woven artefacts.

← ↗ *Ensete ventricosum*
ROYAL BOTANIC GARDENS, SYDNEY,
NEW SOUTH WALES (AUSTRALIA)

Ensete ventricosum →
ST-JEAN-CAP-FERRAT
(FRANCE)

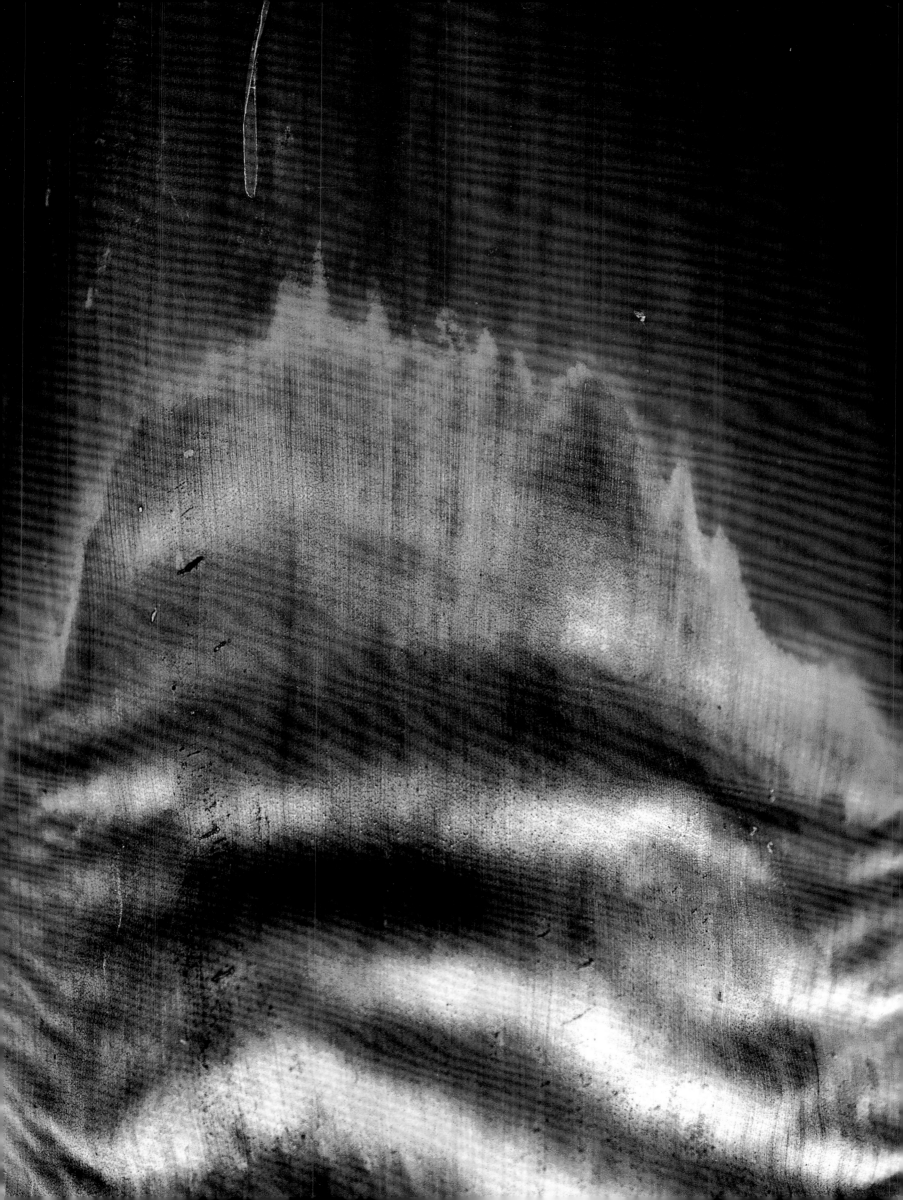

↗ *Ravenala madagascariensis,* symbol of the Great Red Island of Madagascar.
PARC NATIONAL DE RANOMAFANA (MADAGASCAR)

TRAVELLERS' TREE

Ravenala madagascariensis

The true emblem of Madagascar, the travellers' tree symbolizes the exotic and the tropical in most parts of the world. It is found principally in its natural habitat on the east coast of the island (sometimes known as the Great Red Island, on account of the red soil). Botanically it is a close cousin of the bird-of-paradise *(Strelitzia sp.)* and many people confuse it with a palm tree or banana plant. Water accumulates at the base of the long leaf stems. Even when stagnant and teeming with insects, this reservoir has saved the lives of travellers lost in the Madagascan forest, hence its common name. The beautiful long leaves, arranged in the typical fan shape, as well as the false trunk, are used in the construction of the island's traditional houses. With their unusual turquoise flesh removed, the starchy seeds are crushed and then cooked in milk.

Ravenala madagascariensis →
PARC NATIONAL DE RANOMAFANA
(MADAGASCAR)

AFRICAN FAN PALM

Borassus aethiopium

Found throughout tropical Africa, particularly in the Sahel region, the African fan palm plays an important part in the lives of many Africans: the sap is used to make palm wine, the fruits and the shoot tips (palm hearts) are used for food, the wood is termite-resistant and its vegetable fibres are used to make mats. Just like the Bismarck palm (a close relative), it has beautiful grey-green fronds, proof of its adaptation to drought. Although it is undeniably very attractive, it is too slow growing to be widely cultivated.

↗ *Borassus aethiopium*
Mounts Botanical Garden,
West Palm Beach, Florida (USA)

↗ *Borassus aethiopium*
Mounts Botanical Garden, West Palm Beach, Florida (USA)

↗ *Borassus madagascariensis*
Fairchild Tropical Botanic Garden, Coral Gables, Florida (USA)

BISMARCK FAN PALM

Bismarckia nobilis

In some very dry zones in the southern central part of Madagascar, the annual fires of the savannah have created a fascinating landscape of plants, dominated by the Bismarck fan palm. A genus with just one species, found solely on the Great Red Island, it acquired its noble name on account of its majestic character, its huge palm fronds with their white waxy coating and the ease with which it can be cultivated. The German botanists who discovered and named it at the end of the 19th century wanted to honour the first Chancellor of the German empire, Otto von Bismarck.

↗ *Bismarckia nobilis*
ISALO NATIONAL PARK (MADAGASCAR)

FONY BAOBAB

Adansonia rubrostipa

The name *Adansonia* honours the French botanist Michel Adanson who studied African flora and discovered this legendary tree in the 1750s. Madagascar has seven or eight known species, of which six are exclusive to the island. While some species are known for their majestic stature (*A. grandidieri*), others are just the opposite, such as this one, the fony baobab, the smallest of the baobabs. It grows on the west side of the island in the prickly bush and the dry deciduous forests. Its bottle-shaped trunk, fine ochre-tinted bark and round, velvety fruit (rich in calcium and vitamin C) make it easy to identify. The bark has medicinal properties and is used as to cure stomach upsets and to induce lactation.

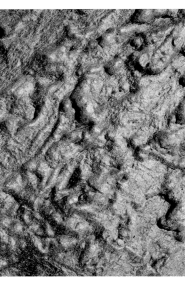

↗ *Adansonia digitata*
KRUGER NATIONAL PARK (SOUTH AFRICA)

↗ *Adansonia grandidieri*
MORONDAVA (MADAGASCAR)

←
→ *Adansonia rubrostipa*
RÉSERVE DE RÉNIALA,
MANGILY (MADAGASCAR)

↗ A striking population of *Pachypodium geayi* in the dry scrub on the island. Tsimanampetsotsa National Park (Madagascar)

MADAGASCAR PALM

(Apocynaceae Family)

Pachypodium geayi

The genus *Pachypodia* consists of 17 species, of which 12 are endemic to Madagascar. Its name means 'thick foot', referring to the swollen trunk, which is bottle shaped in some specimens. The Madagascar palm, with its white flowers and long trunk is the star of the dry deciduous forests of south-western part of the island. Its local name 'vontaka' means 'star of the Savannah'. It can reach 10m (33ft) in height and develops an attractive shape. It is a succulent that is perfectly adapted to drought: the spines and the downy leaves help to limit water loss, while the spongy tissues can store water well, and the white bark of the adult specimens helps to reflect the sun's rays. It was discovered by the French botanist, Martin Francois Geay, during his travels to Madagascar at the beginning of the 20th century.

Evolution of the trunk over decades

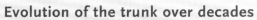 The fall of the spines and the folding of the bark.
Pachypodium geayi ARBORETUM D'ANTSOKAY, TOLIARA (MADAGASCAR)

EUPHORBIA PLAGIANTHA

Euphorbia plagiantha

The genus *Euphorbia,* with nearly 2,300 species, is one of the most diverse in the world. Just like the rubber tree, which belongs to the same family, it is characterized by its milky sap (latex). In certain perennial euphorbias, the sap has purgative and wound-healing properties. Its first recorded use was by Euphorbos, the doctor to King Juba II of Numidia, an ancient province of the Roman Empire. Nevertheless, in other species the sap can be a major irritant and even dangerous. Madagascar abounds in euphorbias – this beautiful tree-like species is endemic to the south-western part of the island and is known locally as fiha ('fish' in Malagasy). It is a coral-shaped species, with a ball-shaped head resembling a coral reef, and with bark that peels in the form of golden, papery curls. Its species name *plagiantha* refers to the 'sideways flowers' which grow at an oblique angle on the shoots.

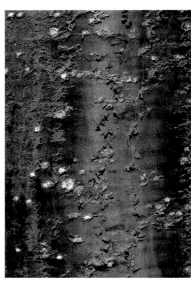

↗ *Euphorbia pervilleana*
RÉSERVE DE RÉNIALA, MANGILY
(MADAGASCAR)

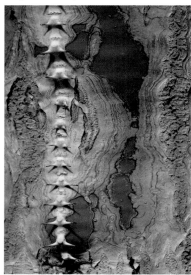

↗ *Euphorbia cooperi*
JARDIN BOTANIQUE
DE LA VILLE DE LYON (FRANCE)

←
→ *Euphorbia plagiantha*
in the prickly bush.
TSIMANAMPETSOTSA NATIONAL PARK (MADAGASCAR)

PAPERBARK CORKWOOD

Commiphora marlothii

Belonging to the same family as the incense tree (*Boswellia*), the corkwoods produce an aromatic resin, of which the best known is myrrh (*C. myrrha*). Its common name, corkwood, refers to its light, supple bark, which also serves as floats for the local outrigger boats. It grows in the dry, rocky areas of south-east Africa. Like many other *Commiphora* species, it has adapted well to very difficult conditions. In the dry season, it loses its leaves to help avoid water loss through transpiration. Then it is the turn of the new green bark, rich in chlorophyll pigments, to take on the job of photosynthesis. The fleshy roots, once chewed, are thirst-quenching and the edible fruits are sometimes made into jams.

→
← *Commiphora marlothii*
on the cliffs of Soutpansberg.
LIMPOPO [SOUTH AFRICA]

Myrrh Trees

The genus *Commiphora*, like its close cousin *Boswellia*, belongs to the renowned family *Burseraceae*, of which it is the major representative with 170 species. You find these trees with their papery, richly coloured bark in Africa, Madagascar, the Arabian Peninsula and the Indian sub-continent. *Commiphora* means, in Greek, 'carrying resin', of which the best known is myrrh, used in medicine, perfumery and religious rites.

1. *Commiphora guillaumini*
   KIRINDY FOREST (MADAGASCAR)

2. *Commiphora arafy*
   KIRINDY FOREST (MADAGASCAR)

3. *Commiphora aprevali*
   RÉNIALA RESERVE
   MANGILY (MADAGASCAR)

4. *Commiphora pyracanthoides*
   LIMPOPO (SOUTH AFRICA)

5. *Commiphora marlothii*
   LIMPOPO (SOUTH AFRICA)

6. *Commiphora mollis*
   LIMPOPO (SOUTH AFRICA)

7. *Commiphora ornifolia*
   SOCOTRA (YEMEN)

8. *Commiphora monstruosa*
   TSIMANAMPETSOTSA NP (MADAGASCAR)

9. *Commiphora* sp.
   SANAA REGION (YEMEN)

QUIVER TREE

Aloe dichotoma

This tree aloe grows in the rocky, dry regions of south-west Africa (Namibia and South Africa). In extremely dry conditions, the vegetative organs of the plant provide a reservoir of water. The tree has a short, stout trunk, covered with golden-brown scales, and a crown composed of a rosette of branches that are much divided. In the winter (June to July) the yellow flowers are a great source of nectar to a range of wildlife: birds, baboons, insects and so on. The bush men take the young branches to use as quivers for arrows, hence the common name, quiver tree. The big trunks of dead trees are hollowed out to serve as natural fridges, as the corklike tissues of the trunk provide good insulation.

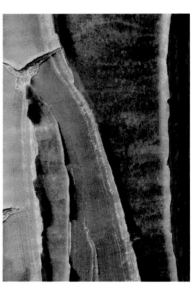

↗ *Aloe dichotoma*
JARDIN EXOTIQUE DE MONACO

↗ *Aloe pillansii*
KAROO DESERT NATIONAL BOTANICAL
GARDEN, WORCESTER (SOUTH AFRICA)

→
← *Aloe dichotoma*
KAROO DESERT NATIONAL BOTANICAL
GARDEN, WORCESTER (SOUTH AFRICA)

NAMIBIAN VINE

Cyphostemma juttae

There are 300 species of *Cyphostemma* in Africa and Madagascar. The Namibian vine with its swollen trunk is a typical succulent of the Namibian plains. During the dry season in winter it loses its leaves and the trunk begins to peel. The young green (and photosynthetic) bark turns white in the summer, helping to reflect the sun. It belongs to the same family as the grape vine, and produces a number of red fruits, although they are not edible. For a long time, the Namibian vine was classified in the *Cissus genus*, but it is distinguished from it by its corolla in the form of an ornate egg timer, its species name coming from the Greek *kyphos* meaning 'ornate' and *stemma* meaning 'crown'. Its Latin name is a reference to Jutta Dinter, the wife of the German botanist who first classified this plant in 1911.

↗ *Cyphostemma currorii*
ETS KUENTZ, FRÉJUS (FRANCE)

↗ *Cyphostemma macrocarpum*
FORÊT DE KIRINDY, MENABE (MADAGASCAR)

→
← *Cyphostemma juttae*
ETS KUENTZ, FRÉJUS (FRANCE)

CANARY DATE PALM

Phoenix canariensis

The real date palm (*P. dactylifera*) is cultivated throughout the world for its sweet fruit, but the Canary date palm, whose fruit are inedible, is nonetheless popular. With its fast growth rate, hardiness and ease of cultivation, it is often grown as an ornamental plant in the countries around the Mediterranean. Its crown, which consists of about a hundred palm fronds, forms a huge ball shape. Pruning them creates a very distinctive lozenge pattern of scales on the trunk. Growing naturally in the Canaries, it was introduced to Nice by Viscount Vigier in 1864. In conjunction with its American counterpart, the Washingtonia, the landscape of the Cote d'Azur has been progressively turned into a giant urban palm house. Its name comes from the Greek, *phoenix*, referring to the Phoenicians who introduced it to the Greeks.

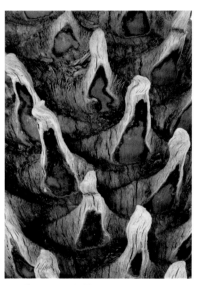

↗ *Phoenix roebellini*
St-Jean-Cap-Ferrat (France)

↗ *Phoenix theophrastii*
Royal Botanic Gardens Kew
Richmond (UK)

→
← *Phoenix canariensis* after pruning
Canet-en-Roussillon (France)

Index of Latin names

↓ *Dracaena cinnabari* SOCOTRA (YEMEN)

credits and thanks

I must thank my family and close friends, who have encouraged and sustained me since I set out on the slightly odd path of exclusively photographing bark, and making a career of it. I must equally thank all those, both near and far, who have helped me to create this book over the course of the last ten years. There are many of you, and your generosity, enthusiasm, knowledge and shared passion for the plant world have given me the energy and the means to fulfil this dream.

Bark: An Intimate Look at the World's Trees

Text and photographs by Cédric Pollet www.cedric-pollet.com
With the exception of p.98 *Eucalyptus coccifera* (Patrick Murray)
and p.70 *Acacia cyperophylla* var. *cyperophylla* (Bruce Maslin)

Originally published in France as *Écorces: Voyage dans l'intimité des arbres du monde*
Copyright © Les Éditions Eugen Ulmer www.editions-ulmer.fr

First published in the English language by
Frances Lincoln Limited
4 Torriano Mews
Torriano Avenue
London NW5 2RZ
www.franceslincoln.com

Copyright in this English edition © Frances Lincoln Ltd 2010
Translation by Susan Berry
With thanks to Simon Toomer, Westonbirt Arboretum

All rights reserved.
No part of this publication may be reproduced, stored in a retrieval system, or transmitted, in any form, or by any means, electronic, mechanical, photocopying, recording or otherwise without the prior written permission of the publisher or a licence permitting restricted copying. In the United Kingdom such licences are issued by the Copyright Licensing Agency. Saffron House, 6-10 Kirby Street, London EC1N 8TS.

A catalogue record for this book is available from the British Library.

978-0-7112-3137-5

Printed and bound in China

1 2 3 4 5 6 7 8 9

Win
GCC >11